The
Equal Rights
Amendment

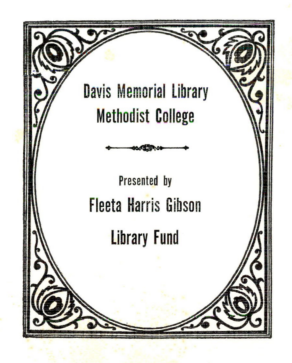

RECENT TITLES IN
BIBLIOGRAPHIES AND INDEXES IN WOMEN'S STUDIES

Women in China: A Selected and Annotated Bibliography
Karen T. Wei

Women Writers of Spain: An Annotated Bio-Bibliographical Guide
Carolyn L. Galerstein and Kathleen McNerney, editors

The Equal Rights Amendment

An Annotated Bibliography of the Issues, 1976-1985

Compiled by
Renee Feinberg

Bibliographies and Indexes in Women's Studies, Number 3

GREENWOOD PRESS
New York • Westport, Connecticut • London

LIBRARY OF CONGRESS CATALOGING-IN-PUBLICATION DATA

Feinberg, Renee.

  The Equal Rights Amendment.

  (Bibliographies and indexes in women's studies,
ISSN 0742-6941 ; no. 3)
   1. Equal rights amendments—United States—
Bibliography. I. Title. II. Series.
KF4758.A1F45   1986   342.73'0878   86-19371
                       347.302878
ISBN 0-313-24762-5 (lib. bdg. : alk. paper)

Library of Congress Catalog Card Number: 86-19371
ISBN: 0-313-24762-5
ISSN: 0742-6941

First published in 1986

Greenwood Press, Inc.
88 Post Road West, Westport, Connecticut 06881

Printed in the United States of America

∞

The paper used in this book complies with the
Permanent Paper Standard issued by the National
Information Standards Organization (Z39.48-1984).

10 9 8 7 6 5 4 3 2 1

TO ELLEN MORAN BOLGER

Start now. The child inside you you've disowned--oh let the child out now to play. Let her out, and let her be as angry as she wants. Let him out, and let him be as loving as he wishes. Let the old woman, the old man so patiently waiting to be their own free selves out now, let their wisdom and compassion tell you what you've always known you never thought you knew. Let out the curiosity and desire. Let the sexless, raceless, ageless brain and heart speak and sing, furious and insistent on celebrating this brief life, on making it more beautiful in color and fragrance and lovely, random, disordered sanity so as to attract the humming consciousness of the universe into a cross-pollination. Start now.

Robin Morgan

The <u>Anatomy</u> of <u>Freedom</u>.
(Doubleday, 1982). p. 323.

Contents

Preface

This bibliography on the Equal Rights Amendment is a sequel to The Equal Rights Amendment: A Bibliographic Study. by Anita Miller and Hazel Greenberg (Greenwood, 1976). The purpose of this bibliography on the ERA is to provide a record of the literature since 1976, the date of the previous bibliography published by Greenwood Press. Since 1976, fewer than forty monographs have appeared on the ERA, most of them limited in scope and seeking to advance a point of view. Of merit is Nancy McGlen and Karen O'Connor's Women's Rights (Preagar, 1983).

Existing literature on the Equal Rights Amendment is skewed heavily towards federal law and the ratification drive, and this aspect of the literature is covered in Chapters Two, Seven, Eight, and Nine. Information on the impact of the Amendment on education, family life, and the military is limited, as is reflected in Chapters Four, Five, and Six. Also included in this bibliography is a chapter (Chapter Ten) on the television networks' nightly news broadcasts. An entire chapter is devoted to this medium because of the impact television has had on the public's awareness of the Equal Rights Amendment. It is possible that part of the answer for the defeat of the ERA lies in an analysis of television's treatment of the ERA. Television fostered the "other side" and gave ERA's opponents a considerable amount of air time. News coverage strengthened the conservative argument that was cast in simple stereotypes and simple visual images, showing that the ERA violates the tradition of the family and the moral code of a nation, and that defeat would be assured if it were not for the radical fringe of women's libbers. However, the evidence indicates to the contrary that the ERA enjoyed large public support, and ratification efforts were instead blocked by powerful interest lobbies which represented opinions of minority groups.

Bibliographic references are drawn primarily from newspaper and journal articles. Three hundred eighty newspaper references from a data base search of The New York Times, the Wall Street Journal, and the Washington Post are included. Approximately 250 journal articles obtained through manual and on-line searches are also included. Although searching revealed fewer than thirty citations, government documents also provide cogent and readable information. The United States Commission on Civil Rights' The Equal Rights Amendment (June 1981) is excellent. This document outlines the issues that have encouraged the public to support the idea and language of the Amendment, but to shy away from its ratification. Another area of well-reasoned articles appears in law journals.

This bibliography is designed for the college student or beginning researcher. It will be useful to those with access to a college library or other collections supporting an undergraduate library such as a large public library and a law library. The introductory chapter outlines the issues of the Equal Rights Amendment and each subsequent chapter begins with the major citations, of length and substance, which are annotated.   Other citations follow and are listed in alphabetical order by main entry.   This bibliography covers the literature on the Equal Rights Amendment since 1976.   Annotated citations appear first, and are chosen because they are three or more pages in length, are of substance, and state or advance the major arguments or are from interesting sources.   Articles fewer than three pages in length are not annotated.   All government documents are listed in Chapter Two. Newspaper articles are entered by title.   Chapter Ten lists selective television news broadcasts in chronological order.   The time (Central Standard Time) given is the beginning time of broadcast recorded at the Vanderbilt Television News Archive, Knoxville, Tennessee.   The writer followed the Modern Language Association's <u>MLA</u> <u>Handbook</u> <u>for</u> <u>Writers</u> <u>of</u> <u>Research</u> <u>Papers</u> (2nd ed.), with modifications.

ACKNOWLEGMENTS

A grant from the Professional Staff Congress-City University of New York, 1984-1985, enabled Aviva Krumbein and Cynthia Van Hazinga to assist in the preparation of this manuscript.   The grant also allowed for a visit to the Vanderbilt Television News Archives, Vanderbilt University, Nashville, Tennessee.   James Mahoney of the Brooklyn College Computer Center gave unstintingly of his time to the production of the manuscript.

Chronology of the Equal Rights Amendment

1923   The Equal Rights Amendment is introduced to Congress.

1971   U.S House of Representatives approves the proposed ERA.

1972   U.S. Senate approves the proposed ERA.   It is sent to the
        state legislatures for ratification.   Twenty states
        ratify: Alaska, Colorado, Delaware, Hawaii, Idaho,
        Iowa, Kansas, Kentucky, Maryland, Massachusetts,
        Michigan, Nebraska, New Hampshire, New Jersey, New
        York, Rhode Island, Tennessee, Texas, West Virginia,
        and Wisconsin.

1973   Wyoming, South Dakota, Oregon, Minnesota, New Mexico,
        Vermont, Connecticut and Washington ratify the ERA.
        Nebraska votes to rescind.   AFL-CIO reverses its
        earlier stand and votes to endorse the ERA.

1974-76 Maine, Montana, Ohio ratify.   Tennessee votes to rescind.
        Pressure from anti-ERA right-wing groups begins to
        surface in boycott of unratified states.   Representative
        Elizabeth Holtzman (D NY) introduces a bill calling for
        an extension of the ERA deadline.

1981   Ronald Reagan becomes the first president who opposes the
        Equal Rights Amendment.   Betty Ford and Alan Alda
        co-chair NOW's ERA.

1982   ERA dies, failing ratification by three states.

1983   ERA reintroduced in Congress.

States With Equal Rights Amendments
(Or Equivalents)
And Year of Adoption

Wyoming	1890
Utah	1896
New Jersey	1947
Hawaii	1968
Illinois	1971
Pennsylvania	1971
Virginia	1971
Alaska	1972
Colorado	1972
Maryland	1972
Texas	1972
Washington	1972
Montana	1973
New Mexico	1973
Connecticut	1974
New Hampshire	1975
Massachusetts	1976

P-1.   Harrison, C. E.   "A 'New Frontier' for Women: The Public Policy
       of   the   Kennedy   Administration."   The   Journal   of
       American History December 1980: 630-646.

P-2.   Hewitt, N. A.   "The Origins of the Equal Rights Amendment -
       American Feminism Between the Wars."   Annals of the
       American Academy of Political and Social Science January
       1983: 177-178.

P-3.   Myers, M.   "Equal Rights Amendment - Bibliographic Study."
       RQ Reference and Adult Services Division 17.1 (1977):
       74-75.

P-4.   "The Personhood of Women."   Wall Street Journal 24 March 1982:
       26.

P-5.   "Reflections and Perspectives on the Women's Movement in 1976."
       Vital Speeches 15 October 1976: 4.

P-6.   Rossi, A. S.   "Beyond the Gender Gap: Women's Bid for Political
       Power."   Social Science Quarterly 64.4 (1983): 718-733.

P-7.   Sochen, J.   "The Origins of the Equal Rights Amendment -
       American Feminism Between the Wars."   Journal of
       American History 69.2 (1982): 489-490.

P-8.   (Statements   of   the   National   Organization   for   Women).
       Washington, DC, 1981.

P-9.   Steuernagel, G. A.   "The Origins of the Equal Rights
       Amendment."   Polity 16.3 (1984): 506-514.

The
Equal Rights
Amendment

Introduction: The Equal Rights Amendment as a Mainstream Political Issue

After fifty years before the Congress, the Equal Rights Amendment was passed by the Ninety-Second Congress on March 22, 1972, and then submitted to the state legislatures for ratification. Failing to gain ratification by three-fourths of the state legislatures, or thirty-eight states, this amendment failed to become part of the United States Constitution in 1982. The Amendment was unable to obtain the votes of three more states in order to be ratified.

Despite this legislative record, the ERA has long enjoyed widespread popular support. In 1982, both the Gallup Poll and the Harris Survey reported that the nation supported the Equal Rights Amendment by a margin of more than two-to-one. More than 450 major organizations with memberships well over 50 million have endorsed the ERA. Therefore, the majority of voters apparently supports the ERA and favors its passage. This support for ERA demonstrates that it is a mainstream issue and that its ratification is long overdue. The question today concerns whether another nationwide effort should be undertaken to gain ratification for a federal amendment or if organizing efforts should instead be put into the ratification of similarly worded state equal rights amendments. (Indeed, some states have added equal rights amendments.)

The text of the proposed Equal Rights Amendment was as follows:
Section 1. Equality of rights under the law shall not be denied or abridged by the United States or by any State on account of sex.

Section 2. The Congress shall have the power to enforce, by appropriate legislation, the provisions of this Article.

Section 3. This Amendment shall take effect two years after the date of ratification.

In an article entitled "The Equal Rights Amendment: A Constitutional Basis for Equal Rights for Women," [Yale Law Journal, 80:5 (1971): 872-985] Yale Law School students Barbara Brown, Gail Falk, and Ann Freedman, with the assistance of Professor Thomas Emerson, argue the constitutional basis for the Equal Rights Amendment. The authors call for an absolute standard of equal rights that would promote a unitary system of equality for all, to replace the present system of dual rights and responsibilities that imposes a different set of values on men and women. The article concludes that this duality defines women as separate and, consequently, inferior in our male-dominated society.

Brown et al. contend that the separate place of women in the legal system is so pervasive that neither the expansion of the equal protection clause of the Fourteenth Amendment, nor piecemeal legislative reform would achieve equal rights for women. To achieve equal rights under the law, no less than a constitutional amendment is necessary. Such an amendment will work as a signal to all levels of government of a national commitment to end sex discrimination. The fundamental legal principle embodied in the Equal Rights Amendment is that "sex is not a permissible factor in determing the legal rights of women, or of men."

> The fact that in our present society members of one sex are more likely to be found in a particular activity or to perform a particular function does not allow the law to fix legal rights by virtue of membership in that sex. In short, sex is a prohibited classification. (See Chapter 2, 2-26, Brown et al., p. 889).

Gender, it is asserted, must not matter in any area of legal rights. It must not matter in determining the right to a minimum wage, the right to custody of children, the right to serve in the armed forces, etc. The constitutional commitment to the right of the individual to pursue life, liberty, and happiness is currently limited for women. To prevent individuals from fulfilling their potential is to judge one group as inferior and to confer on that group second class citizenship. Since legal rights are interwoven with economic and social rights, the denial of political equality for women subsequently results in their economic and social inequality as well.

THE EQUAL RIGHTS AMENDMENT AND FEDERAL AND STATE LAW

When the House of Representatives passed the proposed Equal Rights Amendment to the United States Constitution on October 12, 1971, and the Senate on March 22, 1972, the Congress allowed seven years for the Amendment to be ratified by the states. In 1978, Congress extended that deadline to June 30, 1982. One way of understanding the probable impact of the ERA is to examine the intent of Congress. Both the hearings before the House Committee on the Judiciary of the Ninety-Second Congress, "Equal Rights for Men and Women" (H.R. Doc. No. 359, 92nd Cong., 1st Sess., 1971) and those before the Senate Committee on the Judiciary (S. Doc. No. 689, 92nd Cong., 2nd Sess. 6-7, 1972) record congressional intent. They document the failure of the equal protection clause of the Fourteenth Amendment to prohibit sex discrimination and admit that the Supreme Court, bound by previous discriminatory decisions, continues to discriminate against women.

For example, the testimony of Senator Birch Bayh (D. IN), a leading proponent of the ERA, calls for a constitutional amendment because people recognize the Constitution as the supreme law of the land.   He argues that equality before the law does not mean sameness, and that the purpose of the Amendment is to require the law to deal with women as individuals and not as members of a sex stereotyped group.   The sexes are not identical and the states would not be prohibited from requiring reasonable separation of the sexes, such as in public toilets and sleeping accommodations.   Restrictive discriminatory labor laws would be invalid, but those that conferred real protection would be extended to both men and women; the wage earner would have to support the spouse at home; both men and women would be eligible for the draft; and neither state abortion laws nor laws regarding homosexuals would be contravened.

During the campaign for passage of the ERA, Congress rejected all attempts to modify the language of the Amendment such as those of Senator Sam Ervin (D. NC), a leading opponent of the Amendment. Ervin sought language which would secure extraordinary privacy rights, protect widows, exempt women from combat, require fathers to support their children, and criminalize certain sexual behavior.   Ervin charged that the ERA made men and women into identical legal beings with the same rights and subject to the same responsibilities.   Senator Bayh agreed in part: men and women will be subject to the same rights and responsibilities, but on the basis of individual talents and skills rather than sex.   However, Congress wanted a simply stated amendment which would not recognize any distinctions nor create separate classes of men and women nor limit the Supreme Court's ability to interpret it broadly.   The language of the ERA reflects Congressional understanding of previous discriminatory legislation justified as protecting women.   Congress did not want to provide any loopholes for states to pass new discriminatory legislation and call it protective.

In the House hearings, Representative Ella Grasso (D. CT) speaks of how hard it is to look forward to the upcoming bicentennial celebrations when the legal system looks back to English common law that does not recognize women as legal entities.   Representative Herman Badillo (D. NY) calls for an end to the double standard in society. Representative Claude Pepper (D. FL) states that the protective restrictions have the effect of maintaining women in dependent status before the law.   According to Representative Robert Kastenmeier (D. WI), a constitutional amendment is required to undertake fundamental changes in government.   "Women are citizens without the full rights of citizenship....Nothing short of total equality of rights for all individuals--one system of equality for all--is acceptable." (H.R. Doc. No. 359, 92nd Cong., 1st Sess., 1971)

Congress has proposed the Equal Rights Amendment to supercede the dual system of law which treats men and women differently. Opponents argue that Congress seeks to eliminate privacy rights, to require unisex toilets, and to deny divorced women alimony and child support.   They argue that ERA would demand outside employment for women who choose to be homemakers and draft women, which would destroy the family.   Opponents claim that ERA would promote abortion and homosexuality and that male sex crimes would go unpunished. They charge ERA with violating the religious definitions of male and female roles. Phyllis Schlafly, a leading opponent, argues that the ERA does not put women in the Constitution, but sex. (STOP ERA, 1978-1979). And the Reverend Jerry Falwell contends that the ERA is a "Satanic Attack Upon The Family And The Bible...[it] strikes at the foundation of our entire social structure...[and is] not...[a] political issue, but a moral one." (See Chapter 2, 2-5, Childs, 1982, p. 4)

Speaking to the concerns of the opponents of ERA, Representative Grasso states that some people fear that men and women would lose their femininity and masculinity in achieving equality of opportunity and responsibility. "This is simply not so. What women are striving for today is to gain their humanity and not lose their femininity."

The ERA rests on the premise that distinctions between men and women are legally irrelevant with three exceptions: the right of privacy, the rights derived from unique physical characteristics, and the power of the state to regulate cohabitation and sexual activity of unmarried persons in public accommodations.

Good and ample evidence of what a fully enacted ERA means is illustrated by the seventeen states that have equal rights amendments in their own constitutions (See Chapter 2, Brown 1977). For example, state courts recognize the value of a mother's services. In Texas the duty of both parents to provide child support does not require equal monetary contributions. If the mother, for example, is a housewife, her services are counted in kind. Under Pennsylvania's equal rights amendment, a divorced mother is not required to go to work because the courts recognize the value of her homemaking services. State equal rights amendments have not mandated abortion funding. In Massachusetts and in Connecticut, where Medicaid restrictions on abortion were challenged under the states' amendments, the courts ordered funding on privacy and other grounds. Same-sex marriages have not become legal under state equal rights amendments. In Washington, a statute prohibiting homosexual marriage was upheld under the equal rights amendment. State equal rights amendments do not protect male criminals in sex crimes. (Rape does not go unpunished because women cannot commit it.) And such states as Colorado have rewritten their criminal assault laws in neutral language in order to comply with their state's equal rights amendment.

Other states without equal rights amendments, nevertheless, have rewritten family and marital laws, labor laws, criminal laws, and education laws to make them gender neutral. But the states' records on equal rights are uneven. Virginia still excuses women from jury duty; Illinois and Maryland limit women's ability to establish credit; Texas recognizes a breach of promise to marry; Pennsylvania's courts have ruled inconsistently on extending the common law duty of child support to the mother. The adoption of state equal rights amendments does not produce a consistent effect.

In New York State, the proposed state equal rights amendment failed in the state Senate, causing Madeline Kochen of the New York Civil Liberties Union to write "Will Equal Rights Ever Prevail?" (See Chapter 2, 2-5, Kochen). Arguing against the piecemeal legislative approach to ending sex discrimination, she recommends passage of the amendment. The amendment would authorize the legislature to adopt a systematic, comprehensive approach to eliminate sex-based legal burdens and to address sex-based social and ecomonic problems. A state equal rights amendment would not invalidate veterans' preference laws, interfere with abortion rights, require homosexual marriage, outlaw discrimination by private or religious groups, prohibit separate restrooms, or interfere with the military, as these are matters of federal law.

Section 1 of the proposed federal ERA limits state action and requires states not to deny or abridge equal rights on account of sex. The states have jurisdiction only in matters of a governmental or quasi-governmental nature. Private actions by individuals or by groups of private individuals do not fall into this jurisdiction. The impact of the ERA on state law therefore may follow the course of the impact of the Fourteenth Amendment. Litigation under the Fourteenth Amendment has found that the state does not have the power to regulate private educational institutions, religious groups or churches, banks and savings and loan associations, insurance companies, private clubs, or public accommodations. Whether the dimension of state action under ERA would be limited similarly can only be decided through litigation.

THE EQUAL RIGHTS AMENDMENT'S IMPACT ON EMPLOYMENT, RETIREMENT, AND INSURANCE

By the year 2000 women will earn only 74 percent of men's income ("Women's Near-Liberation," Chapter 3). Yet, current trends indicate that women will no longer be wives, mothers and sometime workers but "workers, mothers and wives, in that order....Later marriage, smaller families, rising divorce and remarriage rates, longer life spans, and changing economic conditions have all driven women out of the home and into the paid work force. Today, the average 20-year-old woman can expect to spend close to 30 years in the paid labor force...be self supporting... [help] support her children and be responsible for her retirement and old age." (See Chapter 3, "Worker, Mother, Wife," 1984, p. 1-4)

The composition of the American work force has changed in the last twenty-five years; women with young children are working for wages. "Today approximately 60 percent of all women ages eighteen to sixty-four are in the nation's paid work force, a nearly 100 percent increase since 1950." A substantial number of these women are married women with young children, and 14.6 percent are single heads of households. Women work primarily for economic reasons. Seventy-three percent of male heads of households earned less than $20,000 in 1980. Therefore women find it necessary to augment the family income. Women and especially black and hispanic women are six times more likely to live below the poverty line. Women's wages contribute to the economic well being of their families and dual wage earning families are far less likely to end up in poverty.

> Women now constitute more than 43 percent of the Nation's labor force...[their] average earnings are only 62 percent of men's; women continue to predominate in a limited number of relatively low-paying occupations, and women's opportunities for full and equal participation in the economy are still negatively affected by sex discrimination in employment. (See Chapter 3, Congressional Caucus for Women's Issues, 1983, p. 8)

Representative Patricia Schroeder (D. CO) says that "economics is 99.9 percent of the ERA." Despite federal laws stipulating equal pay for equal work, a full time woman worker continues to earn 59 cents for every dollar earned by a male worker, continues to be awarded a smaller share of marital property and receives a lower pension rate. Women will earn less, be seasonally employed and segregated in low paying "female" jobs. Women earn less now compared to men than they did twenty years ago. (See Chapter 3, "ERA Round 2," 1983)

The Equal Rights Amendment's impact on employment would reinforce Title VII of the Civil Rights Act of 1964 and the guidelines established by the Equal Employment Opportunity Commission. It would require equal pay for equal work and fair competition in the job market, reasonable nationwide maternity standards, child care leave, child care facilities, equal medical care benefits, equalized pensions, retirement plans, public assistance eligibility, social security benefits, and workman's compensation insurance.

The Equal Rights Amendment would put an end to the inequities of protective labor laws which are found to be keeping women out of lucrative jobs rather than protecting them from strenuous jobs and arduous night shifts. Title VII guidelines of the Civil Rights Act of 1964 suspended many protective labor laws, but many states continue to carry these laws on the books. Under ERA, all such preferential restrictions will be uniformly dropped unless the protection is found to be just and fair and men are protected equally. Under ERA mandatory maternity leaves would give way to disability leaves for both men and women determined by doctors. Weight lifting restrictions would be made gender neutral; overtime restrictions would be dropped and opportunities for high paying overtime would be extended to both women and men.

In 1981, the United States Commission on Civil Rights again endorsed the Equal Rights Amendment and cited the following beneficial changes: invalidating unwarranted legal restrictions on women's labor force participation; protecting public employees from gender-based employment discrimination; and prohibiting gender-based discrimination in insurance, pensions, and retirement security programs (See Chapter 2, 2-20, U.S. Commission on Civil Rights, 1981). As it exists today, social security discriminates against men and women. A husband has a hard time proving he is his wife's dependent and entitled to her benefits; a wife need not prove dependency when her husband dies-- she is entitled to his benefits automatically. A retired working woman receives less than the average benefit paid to a man. Single and married working women and married non-working women are also discriminated against.

The impact of the proposed federal Equal Rights Amendment would be to strengthen existing prohibitions against sex discrimination in the workplace and to require uniform enforcement of current laws which outlaw bias in wages, fringe benefits, hiring practices, and other conditions of employment. Under the ERA, there would have to be strict review of laws and practices concerning seniority systems, veterans' preferences in public employment, and laws that keep pregnant women from working.

Under an enacted ERA, homemakers would be acknowledged as equal contributors to the family's income, thereby according women economic security during marriage, divorce and widowhood. When alimony and/or support is awarded, the courts would be required to apply gender neutral rules in assessing monetary and non-monetary contributions from both spouses. The courts would recognize the homemaker's non-monetary contributions to the family when dividing marital property and would not force divorced mothers to work to meet their support obligations. The duties of the homemaker would be granted legal and economic recognition. This would force a revision of the Social Security system which currently does not grant homemakers disability protection or survivor benefits.

Present retirement systems do not recognize women's work patterns which demand time out of the work force for child-bearing and child-rearing. In 1980, fewer than 10 percent of all American families had the mother staying at home to rear children. Moreover, with the high incidence of divorce and widowhood, the presumption that the husband will be present to provide for his wife is no longer realistic.

> This presumption of dependency works against all women, especially in the Social Security system. If a husband and wife jointly own a business or farm, benefits accrue in his name. If the wife is disabled, she has no credits on which to seek benefits. Because of the principle of only paying one worker in a couple, a two-earner couple with the same income as a one-earner couple receives lower benefits. In 1979, 2.3 million retired women who paid Social Security taxes were no better off than had they never worked for pay and never contributed to Social Security. The net result is a growing population of elderly, poor women. 85 percent of the elderly poor are single women; 60 percent of them depend solely on Social Security for their income. Yet, in 1983 the average Social Security payment for women 65 or older was $4,475, compared to $5,725 for men. (See Chapter 3, Congressional Caucus for Women's Issues, 1983, p. 12)

It is essential for pension systems, today, to accommodate to women's work patterns and needs in order to provide women a decent standard of living after retirement.

Sex discrimination is rife in the insurance field where insurance companies deny women equitable access to disability, life, and health insurance. "Adequate insurance coverage for American women and their families is of critical importance. Women comprise 43 percent of today's work force. They are the primary wage-earners for 7.7 million single-parent families, but their average earnings are only 59 percent of male wage-earners' incomes." (See Chapter 1, Becton and Moorhead, 1971, p. 48)

The Women's Equity Action League reports that despite higher premiums paid by women, they receive lower benefits than men. (See Chapter 11, S. Hrg. 95-1259, part 1, p. 372-374) Disability insurance does not cover part-time workers, the majority of whom are women or women who work in the home. Women pay different premium rates for life insurance based on different life expectancy tables. The ERA would lower insurance costs. Presently, women pay more than men do for health, disability or annuity coverage, although they pay lower premiums for life and auto insurance. The ERA would guarantee that women be treated not as a group but as individuals whose risks are determined by individual behavior or characteristics more closely related to mortality, morbidity, or casualty experience.

THE IMPACT OF THE EQUAL RIGHTS AMENDMENT ON EDUCATION

Nowhere is sex discrimination more venal than in education, where in the traditional nursery school the doll corner was for girls and the sandbox for boys. In our secondary schools, young women are prepared for lower-paying jobs in the service sector and young men are encouraged to enter the better-paying world of high technology. However, under ERA, important educational changes would take place. Single sex public schools would have to integrate. (This would not be true of single-sex private schools unless they accept government funds.) In athletics, if women are qualified to play on male teams, they would be allowed to do so and vice versa. Single-sex fraternities, sororities and other private clubs and associations at colleges and universities would have to integrate if "public funds were so interwoven with the academic life of an institution as to represent official action." (See Chapter 3, U.S. Congressional Women's Caucus, 1983, p. 10)

The implementation of the Equal Rights Amendment would affect those areas of education which discriminate with public funds. For example, under Pennsylvania's equal rights amendment, suit was filed in 1976 against the prestigious public Central High School in Philadelphia (which has an excellent science program) on the basis of its boys-only policy of admissions. The suit had been denied when it was argued under the equal protection clause of the Fourteenth Amendment.

Since 1972 remedies for sex discrimination in education have relied on Title IX of the Education Amendments of 1972 which prohibit many forms of sex discrimination in schools receiving federal funds. But the application of Title IX is limited. It cannot integrate boys and girls in elementary or secondary schools and it does not cover integration in all sports. If a school choses not to accept federal funds, it is not bound by Title IX. Schools have accepted federal funds without implementing Title IX because Title IX enforcement has been found to be weak and cases are seriously backlogged. (See Chapter 2, U.S. Commission on Civil Rights, 1981)

The decision of the Supreme Court in Grove City College v. Bell, in 1984, limited students' protection against sex discrimination under Title IX. The Court limited the application of Title IX at Grove City College to those areas or departments receiving federal money. In this instance, since only the financial aid program came under Title IX, then, only the financial aid program is subject to Title IX provisions. Grove City College is free to discriminate in other areas. Since most federal funding on a college campus is not designated specifically for a particular program, colleges are now free to accept funds and not comply with Title IX. "In other words, most students will not be protected against sex discrimination for most of their college experience" (See Chapter 4, "Supreme Court Guts Title IX," 1984)

State equal rights amendments have strengthened the rights of women and girls in athletics. In Washington, two sisters were successfully integrated into their high school interscholastic football team after having passed all the requirements, (Darrin v. Gould, 1975). Similar decisions guaranteeing girls the same opportunities as boys in athletics were issued in Colorado, Massachusetts, and Pennsylvania. State equal rights amendments are providing as strong a legal basis for challenging discriminatory school rules and practices as either federal laws, including Title IX, or the equal protection clause of the Constitution.

> State ERA's set a clear standard for courts to sue when reviewing sex discrimination claims. The state constitutional provisions are being held to prohibit sex discrimination in all school activities that involve governmental action. (See Chapter 2, Brown, 1977)

Only seventeen states have equal rights amendments. The federal ERA would allow the courts to take up the issue of sex bias in public education, setting aside such limitations as that recently imposed in the Grove City College decision, to trace where public dollars show up in the campus before discrimination is litigated.

THE EQUAL RIGHTS AMENDMENT AND THE FAMILY

Opponents of the Equal Rights Amendment focus their arguments primarily on the family. They contend that the ERA would force mothers into the labor force, end modesty accommodations, interfere with religious education, and allow same-sex marriages. In actuality, what the Equal Rights Amendment will do is correct inequities that vary from state to state. States have different rules for age of marriage for men and women, different definitions of property rights for married men and women, and different appropriation of rights at the dissolution of marriage. In North Carolina, real property held jointly by husband and wife is "under the exclusive control, use, and possession of the husband. Moreover, the husband is entitled to all the rents and profits produced by this property." (See Chapter 2, U.S. Commisson on Civil Rights, 1981, p. 8). In Oklahoma, husbands have exclusive rights in deciding where the family lives and its style of living. In Georgia, the husband is declared the head of the family and the wife is subject to him. Until 1979, Louisiana legally designated the husband the "head and master" of all marital property.

Under the ERA the property rights of married women would be strengthened. Both Pennsylvania and Virginia have found that under their states' equal rights amendments household goods do not belong solely to the husband nor can there be a presumption favoring one spouse over another in determining ownership of personal property.

The Equal Rights Amendment corrects an inequity in that it recognizes the nonmonetary contributions of the homemaker, and the economic partnership of marriage. A woman's economic contribution equals that of her husband. This change towards equity will require adjustment in marriage and divorce laws, in tax laws, in the Social Security system, and in insurance and pension plans. Currently, women lack basic legal rights over marital property and often lack the ability to establish credit. Courts have backed away from enforcing support obligations during marriage fearing a violation of the privacy rights of families. In the event of divorce or death, a homemaker's lack of basic economic rights often forces families headed by women into poverty. On the contrary, divorced fathers are often better off financially even if they pay child support. The ERA would invalidate presumptions about the extent of individual contributions to the marriage and would ease inequities in divorce.

"The Equal Rights Amendment requires that marriage laws be based on functions performed by spouses within the family instead of on gender." (See Chapter 2, U.S. Commission on Civil Rights, 1981) It does not require that husbands and wives contribute identical amounts of money to the marriage nor to the family upon divorce. Under ERA, alimony and support awards would follow gender-neutral rules which recognize the monetary and non-monetary contributions of both spouses. ERA would not force divorced mothers into the paid labor force. In

Pennsylvania, which has a state equal rights amendment, the state court recognized the rights of the divorced mother to stay home to take care of her children. Her non-monetary contribution was respected. The legal and economic rights of husband and wife are recognized under gender neutral laws: ERA does not require that a husband and wife perform the same functions.

The decisions of the Pennsylvania state courts under the Pennsylvania state equal rights amendment make clear the impact of the Equal Rights Amendment on the family, as in the gender-based alimony law that was struck down in Orr v. Orr (PA. S. Ct., 1979). Sex is no longer a permissible factor in determining the legal rights and responsibilities (Henderson v. Henderson, PA. S. Ct., 1974). The courts have found unconstitutional child custody laws preferring mothers to fathers. Pennsylvania regards child support to be the equal responsibility of both parents according to ability (Berry v. Berry, PA. Super. Ct., 1978). The courts recognize the custodial value of homemaker services and do not require divorced mothers to contribute a paycheck to the child's support (Wasiolek v. Wasiolek, PA. Super. Ct., 1977). The presumption that the husband is the owner of all the household goods is set aside in DiFlorido v. DiFlorido (PA. S. Ct., 1975). Here, the Pennsylvania Supreme Court ruled that household property is held jointly in recognition of the value of the work contributed by the homemaker to the marriage. In real estate holdings, all property has been ruled to be jointly held (Margarite v. Ewald, PA. Super. Ct., 1977). (See Chapter 5, Thomas, 1982)

Under the Equal Rights Amendment, the homemaker receives disability protection for herself and benefits for her survivors. Currently, she receives no protection and no benefits. The assumption is that she does not work. There is no social security coverage for women who divorce before ten years of marriage. If a working woman leaves her job to care for her family, she is penalized. Under the Equal Rights Amendment, the social security system would have to examine its assumptions about women's work. The system could no longer refuse to recognize the value of women's work in the home, the existence of job segregation and lower wages paid to women in employment, and the need for women to step out of the paid labor force to bear and rear children. (See Chapter 3, Congressional Caucus, 1983, p. 6)

The law prohibiting single-sex marriages has been contested in Washington under the state's equal rights amendment. However, the court has upheld the prohibition saying that both men and women are subject to the prohibition and therefore it is not discriminatory (Singer v. Hara, Wash. App. Ct., 1974). The right to separate toilet facilities, dormitories, locker rooms, and showers is protected by the constitutional right of privacy and has been upheld by the Supreme Court in Griswold v. Connecticut (1965). The ERA would not interfere with this independent, constitutional right of privacy. The Equal Rights Amendment would not interfere with religions that are apparently sex discriminatory. Federal and state constitutions protect religion from state interference. The Equal Rights Amendment would not interfere with private discriminatory clubs or organizations.

The Equal Rights Amendment would not interfere with existing laws on abortion. Abortion is a protected right under the constitutional right of privacy (Roe v. Wade, 1973). The Supreme Court did rule, however, that Medicaid funds could be withheld for abortion (Harris v. McRae, 1980). Many states have found this decision to violate due process, equal protection and privacy rights of women, and have ruled that Medicaid funds cannot be withheld. This is true in New York State, a state which does not have an equal rights amendment. When Pennsylvania decided to address the question of whether its equal rights amendment required equal funds for abortion, it found that under equal protection the amendment requires equal funding for abortion. However, it also found that Medicaid funds could not be withheld regardless of the State's equal rights amendment. The Equal Rights Amendment therefore does not interfere with existing abortion rights set by the Supreme Court nor its limitations also set by the Court.

ERA AND THE MILITARY

Opponents of the ERA have attempted to limit the question of women in the armed services to that of women in combat. This reduction fails to credit that the military is the largest employer and educator of young people in the country and that sex discrimination in the military continues unabated and unpoliced. All of the service branches have gender-based policies which deny women entrance and promotion opportunities. These policies deny women the education and training needed to perform in dangerous military situtations when they are placed in combat support units. Women are excluded from college scholarships, veterans' education benefits, preference in government employment, insurance and loan programs, and many defense related highly paid jobs in the private sector. Focusing on the issue of women in combat circumvents the issue of denying women increased opportunities for jobs.

In World War II, more than 350,000 women served in the military: 200,000 in combat as nurses, truck drivers, radio operators, and technicians. Yet they were denied training and promotion on the job and veterans' benefits when leaving the armed services. "In 1977, 73 percent of all authorized military slots were closed to women...because women are prohibited from combat, [although] fully 30 percent of these restrictions were not combat related." (See Chapter 10, S. Hrg. 95-1259, pt. 1, Women's Equity Action League, p. 372-374) In 1983, more than 197,800 women served in the military. Women are denied access to officer training programs, are issued uniforms and equipment that fit so poorly as to constitute a health and safety hazard, and are subject to sexual harassment. Service in the armed forces has always been a means of social mobility. Men and women who serve earn more.

Bearing arms to serve one's country has always been intertwined with the ultimate responsibility of citizens. It is a right and privilege that should be available to everyone. (See Chapter 2, U.S. Commission on Civil Rights, 1981)

The Equal Rights Amendment would end sex discrimination in the military. The Equal Rights Amendment would require the armed services to treat women and men equally. Women would be eligible for the draft and eligible for draft exemptions. At present, men are exempted if they are conscientious objectors, the parents of dependent children, or medically unfit. These criteria would apply to women as well. Presumably, men are assigned jobs within the military because of service needs and individual qualifications: women would be assigned jobs in the same manner. The question of women and the draft exists regardless of the Equal Rights Amendment. It is likely that, in the future, women will be subject to the draft. The Department of Defense (see Chapter 6, 1978) is considering the matter because an all-male military draft registration was invalidated in the Supreme Court case Rostker v. Goldberg (1980). The advent and requirements of an all-volunteer army inevitably would demand an increase in women, currently a highly qualified and neglected force to be used for national defense.

There is no existing proof that women are incapable of performing in combat. Combat, defined differently in the different services, has changed over time; and its definition and rules are a reflection of the times rather than an attempt to protect women. Passage of the Amendment would require women to be assigned combat duties according to their qualifications and service requirements just as men are.

An article in Newsweek (November 11, 1985) questions whether women can be kept out of combat. More women are being trained, employed and integrated into the armed forces than ever before. The increasing reliance on women in the armed services can be explained by a diminishing pool of eligible males, and the Carter administration's decision to build an all-volunteer army, willing to accept a better prepared volunteer. The Reagan administration has attempted to reduce this buildup in female personnel by closing many job categories to women. However, there were not enough trained replacements for these women and their job titles have had to be reactivated. Limitations imposed on women vary with each service, making it even harder to prevent women from participating in combat. The current military policy of training women for jobs they will not be allowed to perform when most needed is indeed a waste of taxpayer's money and a complaint among women in the military. In the unlikely event that the United States should pursue a limited war in Europe, it is estimated that women will be five percent of the casualties and five percent of the prisoners of war. It may well prove next to impossible to keep them out of combat. And how would one define combat in a future war involving nuclear strikes against civilian targets? "Women are going to be in combat no matter where they are," says Brigadier General Mildred E. Hedberg. The range of nuclear devastation will not respect gender.

Major Thomas Hogan, a public information officer at Fort Bragg says, "It's not a question of whether women belong in the Army. Clearly they do. The question is whether America is ready for their daughters to come back home in a body bag the way their sons do." (Newsweek)

RATIFICATION

After passage by both houses of Congress, three-fourths, or thirty-eight, of the states needed to ratify the ERA within seven years, or by 1979, for it to become a constitutional amendment. In rapid succession, thirty-five states ratified the amendment.

Hawaii was the first state to ratify the Amendment, followed by New Hampshire, Delaware, Iowa, Idaho, Kansas, Nebraska, Texas, Tennessee, Alaska, Rhode Island, New Jersey, Colorado, West Virginia, Wisconsin, New York, Michigan, Maryland, Massachusetts, Kentucky, Pennsylvania, and California. Twenty-two states ratified the Amendment in 1972. In 1973, Wyoming, South Dakota, Oregon, Minnesota, New Mexico, Vermont, Connecticut and Washington joined their number. Maine, Montana, Ohio, and North Dakota followed in 1974-1975. In 1977 Indiana ratified the Amendment. By 1977, the total of thirty-five states was reached. Four of these states, Idaho, Kentucky, Nebraska and Tennessee, later voted to rescind approval.

The fifteen nonratifying states include the Bible Belt states of Mississippi, Alabama, Arkansas, Georgia, Louisiana, and Missouri, and the Mormon states of Utah and Nevada. Despite fundamental religious tendencies in the South, opinion on the Equal Rights Amendment does vary among the different religious groups. In the Bible Belt, the Southern Baptist Convention dominates. Former president Jimmy Carter is its best-known congregant and also a supporter of ERA. The Southern Baptist congregations have remained quiet on the issue, unlike the Baptist right fringe and the fundamentalists. Mormon opposition to the ERA is particularly ironic as Mormons historically have been persecuted for polygamy. Mormon women were the very model of strong pioneer women. They were among the first women to vote in the United States, they are well educated and well represented in the professions. Nevertheless, the Mormon Church, strongly opposed to ratification, in 1979 excommunicated Sonia Johnson, a Mormon and an activist on behalf of ERA. On the other hand, the United Methodists have supported the ERA since 1972 and they reflect a sizeable percentage of the population in the states that are reluctant to ratify.

Slim prospects for passage exist in North Carolina, Arizona, Virginia, and South Carolina. Supportors of ERA look to Oklahoma, Florida, and Illinois as states where ratification is still possible. The difficulty of state passage rests on the fact that both houses of the legislature must pass the amendment in the same term.

BOYCOTT, EXTENSION, AND RESCISSION

From 1978-1980, efforts to gain ratification in three states, Oklahoma, Florida, and Illinois, in order to bring the total from thirty-five to the required thirty-eight, often led to economic boycotts. Miami Beach and Chicago felt the effects of cancellations of convention bookings by organizations with strong female representation. Teachers, librarians, and psychologists were among those who cancelled. Although a lower court upheld the constitutionality of these boycotts, the Supreme Court did not review the question of whether such boycotts were illegal and in violation of the Sherman Act. In Illinois efforts to win ratification involving hunger strikes and demonstrations were well covered by network news.

As the 1979 deadline for ratification approached and the ratification drive continued to be stalled at thirty-five states, ERA supporters returned to Congress seeking an extension. With no clear constitutional precedent, the House of Representatives voted to extend the ratification deadline to June 30, 1982. The opposition claimed that this was changing the rules in mid-game, but Representative Elizabeth Holtzman (D. NY) pointed out that there was neither magic nor law in allowing seven years for ratification; Congress could just as easily have picked another number. It mattered only that the issue be relevant and current for the process to continue.

Before ratification of the Eighteenth Amendment, Congress set no time limit for passage. Only since the fifties has Congress been following a seven year limit. Passage of the resolution in October, 1978, marked the first time Congress has extended the ratification period for a constitutional amendment. The Anti-ERA proponents seized the issue of extension and mounted a counter move to rescind in state legislatures where the Amendment had already passed. Idaho, Kentucky, Nebraska, and Tennesssee voted to rescind. The constitutionality of rescission has never been settled by the courts, but the Attorney General denys its applicability. It is argued that allowing for rescission in the matter of constitutional amendments would seriously mock the ratification process.

DEFEAT OF THE ERA IN 1982

Having won support of 72 percent of the population represented by the thirty-five state legislatures which ratified the Equal Rights Amendment, the ERA goes down to defeat in 1982.   The Civil Rights Commission (Chapter 2, 1981) posits a lack of clear understanding about the impact of the ERA.   While the public, including the conservative public, supports the ideas of equal opportunity, equal employment, and equal access to education, it is not clear that this is what the ERA is about.   When the well-organized and well-financed conservative right wing is able to portray the ERA as an attack on the family by the women's movement, and as a thinly disguised effort to advance the rights of homosexuals, abortionists, and atheists; the ERA has rough sledding.

It is clear that a minority has held sway on this issue.   Neither Phyllis Schlafly, the Mormon Church, nor Jerry Falwell command a majority segment of public opinion.   Although they enjoy a lot of air time, are well-organized and funded, and have well-honed formal and informal communications networks, they could only prevent ratification in three states.   Therefore, the vote on the ERA might represent a larger referendum, a referendum on the changes brought about by the women's movement.   So profound have these changes been that it is possible to see the narrow defeat of the ERA as the dying gasp of the traditionalists.   It is a single step backward in a very significant march forward for women's rights: a move to retrench after very important gains.

After its introduction to Congress by the National Woman's Party in 1923, the Equal Rights Amendment divides women and women's groups. Women are concerned about losing the benefits they have won. Certainly protective legislation limiting the working day and stipulating working conditions for women and children was not to be forfeited readily.   Opposition in the House of Representatives was led by Representative Emmanuel Celler (D. NY) sitting on the ERA for twenty years as chair of the House Judiciary Committee.   During the Kennedy administration, the Commission on the Status of Women does not recommend adoption of the Amendment.   President Nixon's advisory committee does, however, recommend ratification.   In 1970, Representative Martha Griffiths (D. MI) forces the Amendment out of the Judiciary Committee and before the full House, and Senator Birch Bayh (D. IN) introduces the ERA in the Senate.

The women's movement has been slow to organize around the Equal Rights Amendment.   The movement consists of different groups with different agendas, some political, some social, some religious.   Seldom in the period of ratification from 1972-1982 has the movement acted with the unity of purpose that the anti-ERA forces marshalled.   Over time the National Organization for Women (NOW) began to give ratification of the ERA top priority.   In 1977, NOW planned a national effort in support of ERA and called for an economic boycott of non-ratifying states. It has organized lobbying efforts, rallies, demonstrations and door-to-door campaigns.

> All of these tactics came too late and generally occurred at the wrong level of government.... This lack of coordinated effective effort, however, was probably just one of several factors contributing to the defeat of the amendment. In fact, had it not been for the activities of anti-ERA groups, like the New Right with its close ties to state legislators and corporate interests, the amendment's chances of passage would have been far greater. (See Chapter 9, McGlen, 1983)

ERA's opponents include business interests whose success depends on the status quo. Insurance companies profit from actuarial tables based on stereotypic assumptions about the life-span of men and women. Cosmetic, houseware, etc., businesses that employ housewives oppose the ERA. The conservative John Birch Society establishes and funds anti-ERA groups in different localities. The Mormon Church and fundamentalist Protestant churches lend their organizational suport to oppose ERA. Once ERA is linked to abortion, the National Conference of Catholic Bishops joins the anti-ERA drive.

The themes underscored by the opposition have been that the ERA is anti-family, that it attacks states' rights, and that it is a nightmare for constitutional interpretation. It is unfortunate that this misinformation and erroneous linking of ERA to conservative fears about the demise of traditional family life have not been countered successfully. The language of the Amendment parallels the language of other constitutional amendments in its simplicity and succinctness. The meaning of the language is detailed in the legislative history of the Amendment, and is reported both in the congressional hearings and Brown et al. (Yale Law Journal 80.5, 1971: 872-985). Nevertheless, misleading and false interpretations about the impact of the ERA continue to surround the Amendment and strengthen the opposition. As in the matter of abortion rights, the Equal Rights Amendment has been politicized and is no longer considered a constitutional rights issue but a moral issue concerning the future of traditional values and the nuclear family.

TELEVISION NETWORK NIGHTLY NEWS BROADCASTS

The nightly news broadcasts of ABC, CBS, and NBC during the ratification years frequently reduce coverage of the issues around the Equal Rights Amendment to dramatic confrontations over ratification. Coverage emphasizes the stalling of ratification efforts after the relatively swift ratification by thirty-five state legislatures.

Once the focus is narrowed to a matter of ratification by three states and, once this ratification drive fails, ERA becomes--in the mentality of television--a sign-post for the slowing down of the women's movement. ERA equals ratification equals women's rights, an easy equation. It is the kind of equation television encourages. Television is a visual medium and relies on graphics and film clips supported by brief narrative commentary. The ERA lacks inherent visual drama, so television creates drama to make its point. It has equated the issues of ERA with the struggle for ratification, using the STOP-ERA movement as its anointed opposition.

Television has helped keep Phyllis Schlafly's STOP-ERA movement before the public's eye. But if Phyllis Schlafly had not been around, some other colorful figure would probably have been found to dramatize the very powerful institutional forces at work to defeat ratification in the necessary three states. Television reduces the national debate over equality of rights for women under the Constitution to a contest which women lose. Although the debate over ratification is presented accurately, it is unfortunate that the nightly news broadcasts choose not to use their full powers to inform the public on the range of issues raised by the ERA.

Television's ability to influence the news is furthered by the placement of an item in the newscast. News items about the ERA are often placed at the broadcast's end. They are not long, seldom running over two minutes, and are often only twenty-second news items. From the beginning, news items on the ERA run next to items on abortion, probably constituting the women's issues segments of the broadcasts. There is no doubt that the abortion issue fueled the ERA debate, making it much more bitter and divisive. However, there are only a handful of negative reports on the ERA and some graphics of questionable inference. When it begins to look as though ratification efforts are stalled three states shy, most anchorpersons prematurely sound the deathknell for the Amendment. They remind viewers of ratification defeats and of the divisiveness of the ERA. One wonders if a more optimistic outlook might have helped to move the bandwagon. Did this pessimism predetermine any outcomes?

With the exception of Illinois and, possibly Oklahoma and Florida, it is very unlikely that any other state will ratify. However, the ratification of the Amendment by thirty-five states, no small achievement, is underplayed by newscasters. The remaining states have a history of not supporting legislative reform, tending to be dominated in the southwest by the Mormon Church and in the south by fundamental Protestant sects, both of which hold traditional views on social roles and seek to maintain the status quo.

News broadcasters have not discredited proponents of ERA. Those who speak for ERA are articulate, reasonable, and conservative in dress and manner. There has been no attempt to present supporters of the ERA as members of a militant fringe, as "libbers".

On the other hand, hearing Phyllis Schlafly proclaim that "we will not send our daughters to fight our nation's wars," makes one wonder at the dispatch with which she is willing to send our sons. But what a potent, sinister reference to a nation that saw its sons come home in body bags from Vietnam. Senator Sam Ervin's film clip is no kinder, even though he certainly has friends on the nightly news who introduced his anti-ERA statements with anecdotes about his life in retirement. The contrast is chilling between Sonia Johnson's eloquent defense of her support for the ERA and of herself against charges of heresy and the dry bureaucratic statements that are made by the official spokespeople for the Mormon Church about her trial. Television has captured all of this.

CONCLUSION

The guiding principle of the Equal Rights Amendment is that sex is not a factor in determining a person's legal rights. The law would have to consider men and women as persons with individual attributes and not as males or females. The 1982 defeat of the Equal Rights Amendment has dealt an enormous blow to women's quest for equality before the law, as well as an enormous blow to the women's movement. Because of this defeat, the legal pursuit of equal rights cannot be holistic but must procede piecemeal as case after case is brought against laws, policies, and practices that discriminate against women.

In January 1983, the Equal Rights Amendment is introduced again in both the House and the Senate and is referred to the Judiciary Committee. In 1984, with Senator Strom Thurmond (D. SC.) as chair, the Senate Committee on the Judiciary holds hearings on the impact of the Equal Rights Amendment in consideration of the joint resolution reintroducing the Amendment (See Chapter 11, S. Hrgs 98-1259, parts 1 and 2). Most of the testimony argues that the Equal Rights Amendment will have an adverse impact on education, military policy, veterans' rights, and family law; it will extend federal power over state authority; and it will encourage abortion funding and homosexual rights.

Senator Orrin Hatch (R. UT) speaks about the overall effect of the ERA by quoting Anita Miller, former chairperson of the California Commission on the Status of Women. (S. Hrgs 98-1259, p. 498-513) Miller states that the ERA "is the single most significant event of this century and will bring about a dimension of change greater than ever before." In addition, Hatch refers to Impact ERA that proclaims that the purpose of the ERA is to "transform the social order" and "to establish a new and radically different period of human relations." (Supra, S. Hrgs 98-1259 Summary ..., p. 105) Senator Hatch's choice of quotations echoes the beliefs of ERA proponents and the fears of its opponents: that the ERA seeks to change the traditional rights and responsibilities of women in the United States with constitutional force.

1 Public Opinion and Party Politics

PUBLIC OPINION

1-1. Becton, Betty Gordon and Betty Belk Moorhead. At Ease with ERA: A Syllabus for Use by Groups Examining the Effects of the Equal Rights Amendment. Washington: American Association of University Women, 1979.

Although polls in 1978 by Gallup, Harris, the St. Louis Globe-Democrat, and People magazine show the majority supports ERA; legislators are opposed. The authors provide this syllabus in the belief that better informed support groups could change this situation.

1-2. Blanchard, Christine G., Judith V. Becker and Ann R. Bristow. "Attitudes of Southern Women: Selected Group Comparisons." Psychology of Women Quarterly 1.2 (1976): 160-171.

This is a study of 100 white, upper middle class, Mississippi women. Questionaires were administered to women belonging to one or more social group (either a social change group, a medical center faculty wives group, a business/professional group or a church group). Questions were directed toward several issues including the Equal Rights Amendment. Those in the social change group and the business/professional group tended to support the Equal Rights Amendment.

1-3. Brady, David W. and Kent L. Tedin. "Ladies in Pink: Religion and Political Ideology in the Anti-ERA movement." Social Science Quarterly 56.4 (1976): 564-575.

Surveying the religious and political beliefs of Texas women who are opposed to the ERA, the authors find that the opponents affiliate with traditional church and political groups and are accurately described as members of the American right wing.

1-4. Brown, Sydney T. "Viewpoints on the ERA: Women Against Women." Journal of Current Social Issues 15.1 (1978): 88-91.

Those who oppose the Equal Rights Amendment include male-dominated businesses, hierarchically organized institutions, some churches, supporters of protective labor legislation, and those who fear the loss of alimony payments and forced return to the labor market.

1-5.   Gibb,   Gerald D. and James R. Bailey. "Attitude toward Equal Rights Amendment Scale: An Objective Measurement Tool of Attitudes Toward Equal Rights Legislation." Psychological Reports 53 (1983): 804-806.

The authors developed a scale to measure attitude towards the Equal Rights Amendment and administered it to over 250 men and women from diverse social backgrounds. They found that women were significantly more favorably disposed toward the Amendment than men, however the attitude of older women was less favorable to the Amendment.

1-6.   Gibb,   Gerald D. and Thomas T. Lambirth. "Who Are the Equal Rights Amendment Defenders and Opposers." Psychological Reports 51.3 (1982): 1239-1242.

In analyzing attitudes of college students toward the Equal Rights Amendment, undergraduate males are significantly less favorable towards its passage than undergraduate females. Establishing the categories of masculine and feminine within both male and female respondents, the authors conclude that the "masculine" males are most opposed to the ERA, while the "masculine" females appear to view it most favorably.

1-7.   Gill,   Sandra Kay. "Supporting Equality for Women: An Analysis of Attitudes Toward the Equal Rights Amendment." DAI 43 (1982): 2108A. University of Oregon.

Applying Marxist feminist theories, Gill analyzes a national sample surveyed in 1977. She finds that women who oppose the ERA are more likely to be conservative, affilliated with fundamentalist religions, strongly religious, married or widowed residents of non-urbanized areas, white, and working class. Women who identify as feminists support the ERA. Men who oppose the Amendment are more likely to be conservative, white, and married to full-time homemakers.

1-8.   Hansen,   Susan B. et al. "Women's Political Participation and Policy Preferences." Social Science Quarterly 56.4 (1976): 576-590.

This study examines "the relationship between women's political involvement and opinions on issues of direct concern to women." After finding that "active participants are likely to support equality for women," the authors examine how this effects ERA legislation and ratification in individual states.

1-9. Himmelstein, Jerome L. and James A McRae. "Social Conservatism, New Republicans and the 1980 Election." Public Opinion Quarterly 48.3 (1984): 592-605.

As a result of their study of national election data, the authors dispute that voters from the lower and middle classes shifted to President Reagan. Social conservatives who are strongly opposed to abortion and the ERA, are deeply religious, and are wary of the federal government; supported Reagan. Himmelstein and McRae ask if these social conservatives are the emerging "neopopulist" constituency of the right wing in American politics.

1-10. Huber, Joan, Cynthia Rexroat and Glenna Spitze. "A Crucible of Opinion on Women's Status: ERA in Illinois." Social Forces 57.2 (1978): 549-565.

Based on a telephone sampling conducted in 1976 and 1977, the authors find that the way in which respondents viewed the effects that the passage of the ERA would have on their lives had a more significant effect on their opinion of the Amendment than did their socio-economic characteristics. Non-Protestant, highly educated, divorced women support the Amendment. Older Protestant men with nonemployed wives had negative responses, this group percieved the implementation of ERA as most threatening to the status quo.

1-11. Jacobson, Marsha B. "Attitudes Toward the Equal Rights Amendment as a Function of Knowing What it Says." Sex Roles 9.8 (1983): 891-896.

College students seem to have little first hand knowledge about the ERA. A study among female college students shows that there were fewer misconceptions and more positive attitudes toward the ERA when the text of the Amendment was distributed. This suggests that a strategy for ERA ratification should include dissemination of the text of the Amendment.

1-12. Jones, Ethel B. "ERA Voting: Labor Force Attachment, Marriage and Religion." Journal of Legislative Studies January

1983: 157-168.

Jones claims that her review of the literature reveals three reasons for support or opposition to the ERA: "the relationship of voting constituencies to the labor market, to the family, and to organized religion." All of her tests show an "important role in opposition to the ERA by constituencies associated with fundamentalist Christian sects and the Mormon church." Among economic interest groups, "college students are found to be demandors of ratification ... the support of married women for ERA depends upon their labor force status." (p. 167)

1-13.   Meyer, C. F. "Attitudes Toward the Equal Rights Amendment." DAI 40 (1979): 2907A. City University of New York.

Meyer surveyed members of both pro- and anti-ERA groups as to their value orientations and background characteristics. She found that the "lack of consensus for passage of the Equal Rights Amendment stems more from fear that the passage of the Amendment would pose a threat to the American family and moral standards than from a lack of commitment to equality for men and women."

1-14.   "Public Support for ERA Reaches New High." Gallup Report July 1981: 23-25.

Despite opposition from the Reagan administration, 63 percent of Americans polled support the ERA and 32 percent oppose it. In surveys conducted regularly since 1975, support has never exceeded 58 percent. Although there is majority support for the ERA in all major population groups, somewhat greater opposition is found among Republicans, people living in the midwest and south, and among older Americans. Reasons given for opposing the Amendment include: increasing competition between men and women for jobs, equality already exists, women's place is in the home, and women should not be drafted.

1-15.   Sedwick, Cathy and Reba Williams. "Black Women and the Equal Rights Amendment." Black Scholar July-August 1975: 24-29.

The authors are strongly in favor of the ERA and quote a Gallup opinion poll which found 60 percent of black women supported the ERA as did 63 percent of black men. State opinion polls show black support of the ERA to be stronger than that of any other group questioned. Support was 83 percent as compared with 53 percent among whites.   "It is in the interest of all black people to join the struggle for the ratification of the ERA, as a way to advance the conditions of black women."

1-16.   Spitze,   Glenna   and   Joan   Huber.   "Effects   of   Anticipated Consequences on ERA Opinion."   Social Science Quarterly 63.2 (1982): 323-332.

Interpreting the results of their national survey, the authors examine the effect of background factors on the formation of opinion on ERA.   They find that ERA approval is most affected by spouses' opinion and by certain beliefs about the consequences of implementation of the Amendment.

1-17.   Tedin,   Kent   L.   et   al.   "Social   Background   and   Political Differences   Between   Pro-   and   Anti-ERA   Activists." American Politics Quarterly July 1975:   395-408.

Both pro- and anti-ERA groups are comprised of women.   Proponents of ERA tend to be young and more urban and suburban in origin with secular religious outlooks.   Opponents of ERA tend to be in the political arena because of this one issue, are religiously traditional, and are politically conservative.   Neither group is apt to compromise or support middle-of-the-road politicians.

1-18.   "Deep-Seated Fears That Doomed ERA." (Letter) New York Times 13 September 1982: 18.

1-19.   "ERA: The Doubts and the Fears." (Letter) New York Times 1 January 1979: 16.

1-20.   "ERA, Handgun Control, and the Death Penalty." American Bar Association Journal March 1982: 266-267.

1-21.   "ERA's Death and Fear of New Women." New York Times 29 August 1982: IV, 19.

1-22.   Franck, L. and S. D. Carlson. "Some Effects of Women's Rights Demonstrations Upon Attitudes of Nonfeminist Mormons." ED 237439 (1984).

1-23.   Friedan, B. "The ERA - Does it Play in Peoria?" (Betty Friedan's high school reunion) New York Times 19 November 1978: VI, 38+.

1-24.   McCormick, K. A. "Women's Opposition to Women's Movements." North Central Sociological Association (1983): 981+.

1-25.   Mezey, S. G. "Attitudinal Consistency Among Political Elites - Implications of Support for Equal Rights Amendment." American Politics Quarterly 9.1 (1981): 111-125.

1-26.   Mlott, S. R., R. T. Bostick and R. T. Lira. "Dogmatism and Locus of Control in Young Women Who Support, Oppose, or Voice No Opinion on the Equal Rights Amendment." Journal of Clinical Psychology 33.3 (1977): 746-748.

1-27.   "New York ERA Push Gets Mixed Reviews from Women's Groups." Christian Science Monitor 11 January 1984: 4.

1-28.   Prince, E. S. and I. E. Deutchman. "Identity Status in Politically Active Pro and Anti ERA Women." Journal of Mind and Behavior 2.3 (1981): 309-321.

1-29.   "Public Favors ERA by 2-to-1 But GOP Voters Closely Split." Gallup Opinion Index June 1980: 3-4.

1-30.   Swatos, W. H. Jr. and C. McCauley. "Working-Class Sex Role Orientation." International Journal of Women's Studies 7 (1984): 136-143.

PARTY POLITICS

1-31.   Hill, David B.   "Women State Legislators and Party Voting on
          the ERA."   Social Science Quarterly June 1983: 318-326.

                Women have only recently been elected to state
          legislatures, and, like their male counterparts, they are
          voting the party line.   Republican women were found to
          adhere to the party line and cast anti-women votes on
          such issues as the ERA.   Hill says the ERA might be an
          atypical case and women legislators so few in number as
          to cause this behavior.

1-32.   "Advisor to Carter Calls for Defeat of Rights Amendment
          Opponents."   New York Times 29 May 1979: A18.

1-33.   Arieff, I. B.   "1980 GPO Platform Reflects Party Unity Behind
          Reagan: Conservative   ERA,   Abortion   Planks."
          Congressional Quarterly Weekly Report 19 July 1980:
          2005-2008.

1-34.   "Backers of ERA Protest Against Reagan's Stand."   Christian
          Science Monitor 20 January 1981: A2.

1-35.   "Business Group Urged by Carter to Promote Equal Rights
          Proposal."   New York Times 16 May 1980: A19.

1-36.   "Can   Reagan Heal the Breach Over ERA Issue?"   US News and
          World Report 28 July 1980: 18.

1-37.   "Can   the GOP Heal Its ERA Scars?"   US News and World
          Report 21 July 1980: 8.

1-38.   "Democratic Parley in Contrast with GOP's on Feminist Delagates
          and Issues."   New York Times 8 August 1980: A14.

1-39.   "Democrats Invest Heavily in ERA."   Christian Science Monitor
          14 August 1980: 12.

1-40.   Easton, N.   "The Gap in the GOP: The Republicans Gave Women
          the Vote and Were the First to Support ERA."   Savvy
          February 1985: 72-77.

1-41.   Edwards, D.   "Can Reagan Co-Opt the ERA?"   Ms.   June 1982:
          106.

1-42.   "Emotional Issue for GOP: Equal Rights Amendment is Dividing
          Delegates."   New York Times 10 July 1980: A1.

1-43.   "An Enforceable ERA Plank?"   (Editorial)   Christian Science
          Monitor 14 August 1980: 24.

1-44.   Equal Rights Plan Splits Republicans Drafting Platform."   New

York _Times_ 8 July 1980: A1.

1-45.   "Equal Rights: Testing the Reagan Approach." (Editorial) _Christian Science Monitor_ 7 August 1981: 24.

1-46.   "ERA - Yes, but ..." (Democratic Party support for women's rights) _New York Times_ 10 October 1981: 19.

1-47.   "Foot-in-Mouth Syndrome has Democrats Courting Disaster." _Los Angeles Times_ 17 July 1983: IV, 5.

1-48.   "44 GOP Lawmakers Urge Party to Retain Its Equal Rights Plank." _New York Times_ 2 July 1980: A16.

1-49.   Freeman, J. "Republican Politics--Let's Make a Deal." _Ms._ November 1976: 19-20.

1-50.   "Full Platform Unit of GOP Abandons Rights Amendment." _New York Times_ 10 July 1980: A1.

1-51.   "The GOP and the ERA." (Editorial) _Christian Science Monitor_ 1 July 1980: 24.

1-52.   "GOP Foes of Rights Plank Win." _New York Times_ 9 July 1980: A9.

1-53.   "GOP Group Retreats from Backing ERA." _Wall Street Journal_ 9 July 1980: 7.

1-54.   "Group in GOP Hopes to Soften Stand on Rights." _New York Times_ 13 July 1980: I, 15.

1-55.   Hoodbury, N. "ERA and the '84 Elections." _Guardian_ 30 November 1983: 18.

1-56.   "House Whip to Urge GOP to Back Equal Rights Plan." _New York Times_ 12 June 1980: B12.

1-57.   "Hyde Sees Rights Plan Vote as 1984 Issue for Democrats." _New York Times_ 21 November 1983: 8.

1-58.   "Is Equal Rights a Partisan Issue?" (ERA and Democratic Party politics) _Washington Post_ 29 November 1983: A17.

1-59.   "New Co-Chairman Defends GOP Equal Rights Plank." _New York Times_ 12 July 1980: 6.

1-60.   Noah, T. "About Face." (Republican Party) _New Republic_ 19 July 1980: 14-16.

1-61.   "President Pledges Drive for Rights Amendment." _New York Times_ 9 January 1980: A18.

1-62.   "A Reagan Alternative to ERA." (Reprint from the Seattle Times)

Christian Science Monitor 25 August 1981: 24.

1-63.   "Reagan and the ERA." New York Times 8 January 1982: 23.

1-64.   "Reagan Implies He Wants Platform to Drop Equal Rights
        Endorsement." New York Times 21 June 1980: 8.

1-65.   "Reagan Pledges Woman on Court." New York Times 15 October
        1980: 1.

1-66.   "Reagan Session on Amendment is Closed to Men." New York
        Times 14 July 1980: A14.

1-67.   "Reagan Tries for Peace with Supporters of ERA and with Black
        GOP Members." Wall Street Journal 16 July 1980: 4.

1-68.   "Reagan's Platform." National Journal 26 July 1980: 21+.

1-69.   "Right to Support ERA Affirmed by GOP Panel." Wall Street
        Journal 10 July 1980: 32.

1-70.   "Say, Some Republicans Actually Support ERA." New York
        Times 14 October 1980: 23.

1-71.   Walcak, L. "The Damage that ERA Will Do to Reagan."
        Business Week 4 August 1980: 83-84.

1-72.   "White House Reshapes its Approach to Feminists' Issues." New
        York Times 18 October 1980: 7.

1-73.   "Women Comparing Carter and Rivals." (President faulted by
        some groups for not doing enough to push for a rights
        amendment) New York Times 11 November 1979: 25.

2 Federal and State Interpretations of the Equal Rights Amendment

2-1. Avner, Judith. "Some Observations on State Equal Rights Amendments." Yale Law and Policy Review Fall 1984: 144-167.

   Avner examines state ERAs and says that states act as laboratories for experimenting and understanding the impact of an equal rights amendment were it to be enacted on the federal level. State ERAs have encouraged a significant improvement in the legal status of women and have forced the state courts to take a closer and more sympathetic look at the problems confronting women. They have brought women greater equality in family law matters and in education.

2-2. Berger, M.A. Litigation on Behalf of Women. New York: Ford Foundation, 1980.

   How effective is Ford Foundation-funded litigation in promoting the equality of women? The author finds that the Supreme Court under Chief Justice Burger will not advance the rights of women as the Warren Court did for blacks. Title VII litigation is difficult and costly. Title IX litigation is limited by the uncooperaative attitudes of the Supreme Court. Berger concludes that litigation is slow and expensive and, by itself, can not end sex discrimination.

2-3. Bird, Caroline. The Spirit of Houston. The First National Women's Conference. (An Official Report to the President, The Congress, and the People). Washington: GPO, 1979.

   Many issues affecting women were raised at the Conference, including the ERA. The history of the ERA is given here along with a current analysis of ratification strategy.

2-4. Brown, Barbara. Women's Rights and the Law: The Impact of the ERA on State Laws. New York: Praeger, 1977.

   Brown asserts that states have been reasonable in eliminating gender-based restrictions and in extending rights, benefits and obligations to members of both sexes under state equal rights amendments.

2-5. Childs, Marjorie. Fabric of the ERA: Congressional Intent. Smithtown, NY: Exposition, 1982.

   Childs provides quotations from documents on various issues such as privacy, equality, the Fourteenth Amendment, and sex discrimination. She includes such unusual documents as the "ERA, A Satanic Attack Upon the Family and the Bible" (insert accompanying a letter dated February 2, 1978 sent from Faith Partners, Office Box 1111, Lynchburg, VA). In addition, she examines the record of the Ninety-Second Congress and the discussions leading to congressional passage of the ERA.

2-6. "Continuing Controversy Over the Women's Equal Rights Amendment: Pro and Con." Congressional Digest 56 (1977): 162-192.

   This issue features the Equal Rights Amendment, its legislative history, and the arguments for and against ratification. Arguments in favor of the ERA are presented by Senator Birch Bayh, the National Women's Party, the National Organization for Women and Professor Thomas I. Emerson. Those arguing against the ERA include Senator Sam Ervin, the National Council of Catholic Women, the American Conservative Union, and Phyllis Schlafly. Referring to the failure to keep the momentum to ratify the ERA going, NOW says that it "misjudged the conservative right wing's ability to organize against the ERA." NOW charges the conservative right wing used the ERA to rally its waning forces by "sophisticated propaganda and scare tactics. It was a way of keeping their old boy power network intact."

2-7. Cowan, Ruth. "Women's Rights through Litigation: An Examination of the American Civil Liberties Union Women's Rights Project, 1971-1976." Columbia Human Rights Law Review 8 (1976): 373-412.

   Cowen finds that the lack of coordination of women's court cases presents the courts with a haphazard collection of women's rights issues and hinders the realization of equal rights for women.

2-8. Heins, Marjorie. "'The Marketplace and the World of Ideas': A Substitute for State Action as a Limiting Principle Under the Massachusetts Equal Rights Amendment." Suffolk University Law Review Fall 1984: 347-376.

   Heins discusses the passage of the Massachusetts equal rights amendment and its impact on state action.

She finds that the state equal rights amendment would be seen as barring discrimination in public life. "Equality under the law," should mean equality in matters "with which the law commonly deals." (p. 351)

2-9.   Kay, Richard S.   "The Jurisprudence of the Connecticut Constitution."   (Faculty Symposium) Connecticut Law Review Summer 1984: 667-680.

This symposium reviews the case Cologne v. Westfarms Associates, (1984) in which NOW sued for protection under Connecticut state law since the Supreme Court has denied the extension of free speech to private parties in privately owned shopping centers. Kay argues that constitutional law case decisions are political choices as evidenced here.

2-10.   Kochen, Madeline. Briefing Book for the New York State Equal Rights Amendment. New York: New York Civil Liberties Union, 1984.

Kochen prepared this book for New York state legislators to assist them in answering their questions about the impact of a state equal rights amendment. She says that such an amendment would not transform New York into a unisex society nor destroy the family. It would not prohibit private discrimination nor discrimination allowed by religious practices. A state equal rights amendment would not allow homosexual marriage nor interfere with existing laws on abortion.

2-11.   Lewis, Ellen. "Texas ERA." Women's Rights Law Reporter Fall 1977: 51-55.

In Mercer v. Board of Trustees, the Texas Court of Civil Appeals upheld a lower court ruling against John Mercer who sued under the Texas ERA to protest having to cut his hair. Lewis declares this decision as a "classic example of the judicial perversions of ERA." Lewis asserts that this is a violation of the Court's stated willingness to apply judicial scrutiny to sex-based discrimination.

2-12.   Macgill, H. C. "Anomaly, Adequacy, and the Connecticut Constitution." (Faculty Symposium) Connecticut Law Review Summer 1984: 681-707.

This is a discussion of the decision of the Connecticut Supreme Court in Westfarms (1984) in which the Court found that NOW could not enter a suburban shopping mall to gather signatures on a pro-ERA petition. Macgill says that this decision is part of a historical pattern in which the Court has refused to develop free speech doctrine under the Connecticut Constitution.

2-13.   Proebsting, Patricia L.   "Washington's Equal Rights Amendment: It Says What it Means and it Means What it Says." University of Puget Sound Law Review Winter 1985: 461-484.

Washington added an equal rights amendment to its state constitution in 1972. Its existence has strengthened existing state law but, contrary to voter intent, the State Supreme Court has not allowed the ERA to end sex discrimination. It has not followed an absolute standard as has the Supreme Court of Pennsylvania, and has failed to interpret the ERA literally.

2-14.   Reifsnyder, Betsy.   "A Legislative History of the Equal Rights Amendment in the United States Congress." (1982) ED 238785.

This paper summarizes the history of Congressional intent on the ERA from 1969 to 1982. It includes a chronological outline of congressional action, a flow chart of tangential events, and a bibliography.

2-15.   Richette, Lisa Aversa.   "Equity from a Legal Perspective." (1982) ED 215167.

The history of the doctrine of equal protection is reviewed. Opponents to the ERA argue that this doctrine guarantees the rights of women. Richette refers to Title VII of the Civil Rights Act, affirmative action mandates, court cases, and "protective" legislation.

2-16.   Saucier, Peter S.   "The Maryland Equal Rights Amendment: Eight Years of Application." University of Baltimore Law Review Winter 1980: 342-369.

Maryland has had a state equal rights amendment since 1972. The Maryland Court of Appeals interprets its equal rights amendment as absolutely prohibiting gender-based discrimination. The state ERA "has become a prime mover in the area of equal rights." It has marked a sharp break from the earlier slow march toward equality of the sexes."

2-17.   Schlafly, Phyllis   "The Effect of ERA on State Constitutions."
         Policy Review Summer 1979: 55-84.

         The proposed federal ERA would give the federal
         courts, "which include some of the most activist courts in
         the country...a blank check to fill in after ratification."
         State equal rights amendments do not have the power or
         scope of a constitutional amendment; they can't compel
         women into combat.   "Even if all fifty states were to
         adopt a State ERA, their cumulative effect on our unique
         American federal structure and on our methods of
         fighting wars would be miniscule compared to the vast
         changes that would be compelled by the Federal ERA."
         In matters of family law, wherever a state equal rights
         amendment has been in effect, the wives and mothers
         have experienced "the painful effects of ERA. ... Where
         the ERA made a unique constitutional difference, it
         always resulted in a loss to the woman, especially to the
         wife and mother.   In nearly every case in which the
         State ERA changed prior law, women were needlessly
         deprived of longstanding legal rights."

2-18.   Schoen, Rodric B.   "The Texas Equal Rights Amendment After
         the First Decade: Judicial Developments 1978-1982.
         Houston Law Review October 1983:   1321-1368.

         Texas has lived with a state ERA since 1972.   Unisex
         toilets, homosexual marriages, unpunishable sex crimes,
         nonsupport of wives and children, forced employment of
         wives, and sexless Texans: have not shown up.   Schoen
         examines appellate cases under the Texas ERA which has
         taken on a new meaning since the federal ERA was
         defeated.   Texas' ERA has ended sex-based custody
         awards and husband-preferred domicile decisions.   Texas
         has supported an eight-year-old girl's desire to play
         tackle football, equal overtime pay for women, and
         paternal support of illegitimate children.

2-19.   Treadwell, Lujuana Wolfe and Nancy W. Wallace. "Equal Rights
         Provisions: The Experience under State Constitutions."
         California Law Review 65 (1977): 1086-1112.

         Treadwell examines sixteen state court systems where
         the states have added equal rights amendments.   The
         state courts are applying the standard of review of strict
         scrutiny developed under the Fourteenth Amendment
         which allows gender discrimination in instances of
         compelling state interest.   Only Pennsylvania and
         Washington use an absolute standard of review.

2-20.   U.S.   Commission on Civil Rights.   The Equal Rights

Amendment: Guaranteeing Equal Rights for Women under the Constitution. Washington: GPO, 1981.

The Commission endorsed the ERA in 1973. It continues its support of the basic principle of government treating women and men as equal and having equal rights under the law. It analyzes the gap between the reality of the text of the ERA and the myth of meaning surrounding it and finds that there is often strong support for the principle of equality but not for the Amendment. The American Bar Association is quoted in support of the ERA. "No ordinary statute can provide the bedrock protection assured by a Constitutional Amendent. No court decision can provide that protection, for the courts may intepret, but they may not amend the Constitution." (p. 5) This report provides an excellent summary of the probable impact of the ERA on the lives of women.

2-21. U.S. Commission on Civil Rights. Sex Bias in the U.S. Code. Washington: GPO, 1977.

Initially, this was a report by students and faculty of Columbia University Law School (NY) which assessed the status of women under federal law. They recognized women's progress towards equality through legislative revision and the enactment of new laws. Nonetheless, the U.S. Code continues to define distinct spheres of action for men and women. This report examines two areas of law, the armed forces and social security. It concludes that the use of sex-based terminology tends to reinforce the traditional view of women as subordinate.

2-22. U.S. Senate. Constitutional Amendments. Sen. Rept. 94-1373. Washington: GPO, 1976.

This report includes the legislative history and status of the ERA to 1976.

2-23. Washington State. Women's Council. The Needs and Concerns of the Women of Washington State. 2 vols. Olympia, 1979.

This document describes the impact of the federal Equal Rights Amendment in eight areas. The Council recommends that women be brought into parity with men in publicly financed work training programs; that women be appointed to top level positions in all state agencies; that women be brought in to help redesign health and social service programs; that all state laws be enforced to reflect the "spirit and intent of the state ERA;" that the Governor (Dixie Lee Ray) use her influence to accelerate efforts to ratify the federal ERA, etc.

2-24.   Adler,   J.   "The   Westfarms   Mall   Case: An   English   View."
         (Faculty   symposium)   Connecticut   Law   Review   Summer
         1984: 709-729.

2-25.   Anderson, P. "Pennsylvania: ERA in Practice." Ms.   September
         1978: 92.

2-26.   Brown, Barbara, Gail Fink, Ann Freedman and Thomas Emerson.
         "The Equal Rights Amendment: A Constitutional Basis for
         Equal Rights for Women." Yale Law Journal 80.5 (1971):
         872-985.

2-27.   Carver, J.S.   "Women in Florida."   Journal of Politics August
         1979: 941-55.

2-28.   Cohen, M. "Miami Beach: Little ERA." Ms.   April 1981: 19.

2-29.   "The   Constitution Would Be Poorer Without ERA."   Christian
         Science Monitor 3 February 1982: 23.

2-30.   "Cuomo Rights Plan at Odds with Tactic of Women's Groups."
         New York Times 6 January 1984: A1.

2-31.   "Cuomo Vows Fight on Rights Measure." (Tells women he can't
         afford a defeat in effort to pass Amendment in New York)
         New York Times 13 January 1984: A12.

2-32.   Easman, T. L. "Constitutional Rights of Women Under National
         and International Law: Present Standards and Future
         Possibilities."   Santa Clara Law Review 18.2 (1978):
         453-489.

2-33.   "The Equal Rights Amendment: Guaranteeing Equal Rights for
         Women Under the Constitution." (1982) ED 210372.

2-34.   "Equal Rights in Some States."   Washington Post 20 September
         1983:" A14.

2-35.   "ERA: Myth or Reality." GAO Review Summer 1979: 46-50.

2-36.   "ERAs in Practice."   Christian Science Monitor 12 August 1981:
         23.

2-37.   "Evolution, Not Revolution." (States' equal right laws) Time 26
         March 1979: 25.

2-38.   "Evolution of the Amendment."   Congressional Digest June-July
         1977: 164-166.

2-39.   Foster, M. G.   "Eliminating Sex Discrimination in the Law."
         Social Casework 58.2 (1977): 67-76.

2-40.   Freedman, M.   "The Crucial Legal Import of ERA."   Nation 2
        September 1978: 166-168.

2-41.   Gecas, V.   "The Equal Rights Amendment in Washington State."
        (1979) ED 160507.

2-42.   Ginsburg,   R.B.   "All   About   the   E.R.A."   Cosmopolitan
        November 1979:   166-171.

2-43.   Ginsburg, R.B.   "Sex Equality and the Constitution: The State
        of the Art."   Women's Rights Law Reporter 4.3 (1978):
        143-147.

2-44.   Heins,   Marjorie.   "Feminist   Lawyers   Say   They   Will   Look   to
        Courts to Decide Women's Rights Under the Massachusetts
        Equal   Rights   Amendment."   Suffolk   University   Law
        Review Fall 1984: 347-376.

2-45.   "High   Court   Steers   Middle   Course   on   ERA."   Christian   Science
        Monitor 26 January 1982: 3.

2-46.   "Interpreting ERA."   Wall Street Journal 16 May 1979: 1.

2-47.   "Legal   Experts   Say   Plan   to   Outlaw   Sex   Bias   is   Widely
        Misunderstood."   Wall Street Journal 16 May 1979: 1.

2-48.   Logsdon,   L.   and   G.   M.   Barton.   "ERA: The   Issues."
        Psychiatric Opinion 15.8 (1978): 33-36.

2-49.   Medoff,   M.H.   "The   Equal   Rights   Amendment--an   Empirical
        Analysis   of   Sexual   Discrimination."   Economic   Inquiry
        18.3 (1980): 367-379.

2-50.   Mendelson. W.   "ERA, the Supreme Court, and Allegations of
        Gender Bias."   Missouri Law Review 44 (1979): 1-10.

2-51.   "Miami   Tries   to   Lure   Conventions   with   'Little'   ERA."   Christian
        Science Monitor 7 January 1981: 5.

2-52.   Mott, N. A. "An Analysis of Mississippi's Criminal Law Under
        the Equal Rights Amendment."   Mississippi Law Journal
        47.2 (1976): 279-301.

2-53.   National Commission on the Observance of International Women's
        Year.   Equal Rights Amendment, a Workshop Guide.
        Washington: GPO, 1977.

2-54.   New York State Assembly.   Assembly Task Force on Women's
        Issues.   Comparable Worth.   May W. Newburger, Chair.
        Albany, 1983. (Pamphlet)

2-55.   O'Reilly, J.   "State Laws and Equal Rights the Bogus Fear of
        ERA."   Nation 8 July 1978: 45-47.

2-56.   Picker, J. M. "Law and the Status of Women in the U. S."
        Columbia Human Rights Law Review 8 (1976): 311-343.

2-57.   Rosse, J. O. "Equal Rights for Women." Howard Law Journal
        21.2 (1978): 327-420.

2-58.   Sassower, D. L. "Women, Power, and the Law." American Bar
        Association Journal May 1976: 613-616.

2-59.   Schiefelbein, S. "Scholars at Odds." Saturday Review 25 June
        1977: 12-13.

2-60.   Schnitzer, R. "Our ERA Not Theirs." (New York State) Off
        Our Backs January-February 1976: 11.

2-61.   Seligman, D. "Doing Without ERA." (State laws that reflect
        discrimination) Fortune 15 December 1980: 41.

2-62.   Seligman, D. "Moving South on ERA." Fortune 11 January
        1982: 31-32.

2-63.   Simpson, R. W. "A New Look at the Texas Equal Rights
        Amendment." Texas Law Review 55.2 (1977):323-342.

2-64.   "States Test Their Own ERAs." Christian Science Monitor 2 May
        1979: 14.

2-65.   Strong, F. R. "Contributions of ERA to Constitutional
        Exegesis." Georgia Law Review 14 (1980): 389-434.

2-66.   United States Congressional Caucus for Women's Issues. Equal
        Rights Amendment. Washington: Caucus Staff, November
        1983. (Pamphlet)

2-67.   Welch, S. and D. L. Gottheil. "Women and Public Policy: A
        Comparative Analysis." Policy Studies Journal 7.2
        (1978): 258-264.

2-68.   Wheeler, A.M. and M.S. Wortman. "The Roads They Made:
        Women in Illinois History." (1977) ED135699.

2-69.   "Wisconsin Women and the Law." 2nd ed. Governor's Commission
        on the Status of Women. (1979) ED 159090.

2-70.   "Women Okies are Equal." (Editorial) Christian Science Monitor
        30 April 1979: 27.

3 Employment

3-1. Giraldo, Z. I. "Public Policy and the Family: Wives and Mothers in the Labor Force." (1982) ED 212375.

>   In this document chapters 10-13 discuss the problems of implementing the ERA at the state level and its economic impact on family life.

3-2. Grefe, Mary A. "Equity--A Cause for Every Women." (ERA and employment) Graduate Woman March-April 1980: 10-17.

>   Women want equal access to educational and vocational opportunity as well as equal pay. The ERA is the underpinning of the whole action for equity; without it all gains made in this area can be erased by legislative acts of Congress. The American Association of University Women is sponsoring political and educational action to press for the ratification of the ERA at the federal level. It is also coordinating fundraising activities and workshops on the state level.

3-3. Sigelman, Lee et al. "The Curious Case of Women in State and Local Government." Social Science Quarterly 56.4 (1976): 591-604.

>   Looking at employed women in the public sector, the authors are shocked to find that women fare better in the public sector in those states which have not ratified the federal ERA. These states represent traditional political cultures and have a lower median education, as in the south. However, even in the south, women continue to be relegated to lower level jobs.

3-4.   Deakin, D. "Your Job and the ERA." (What will ratification mean) _Dynamic Years_ January-February 1979: 10-12.

3-5.   "ERA, Round 2: Now the Issues are Economic." _Business Week_ August 1983: 92-93.

3-6.   Fineshriber, P. H. "Jobless Insurance Inequities Deepen as More Women Enter the Labor Market." _Monthly Labor Review_ April 1979: 44-45.

3-7.   "Insurance Blamed in Sex Bias." _New York Times_ 2 June 1982: 12.

3-8.   Owens, M. R. "One Path to Guaranteed Jobs: A Constitutional Amendment." _Social Policy_ Summer 1982: 32.

3-9.   Schnack, M. "ERA: What It Will (Won't) Do for Working Women." _Working Women_ November 1979: 46-48.

3-10. U.S. Commission on Civil Rights. _State of Civil Rights 1957-1983_. (The Final Report of the U.S. Commission on Civil Rights.) Washington: November, 1983.

3-11. U.S. Women's Bureau. _A Working Woman's Guide to Her Job Rights_. Washington: GPO, January 1984.

3-12. "U.S. Life Insurers Unopposed to ERA." (Letter) _New York Times_ 9 June 1982: A26.

3-13. "Why Homemakers Have to Have ERA." _Christian Science Monitor_ 27 February 1979: 27.

3-14. "Women's Near-Liberation." _New York Times_ 12 June 1981: A27.

3-15. "Worker, Mother, Wife: the Future of Today's Girls." Hubert H. Humphrey Institute of Public Affairs. University of Minnesota: Minneapolis, August, 1984.

4 Education

4-1. Bers, Trudy Heffron "Perceptions of Women's Roles among Community College Women." Psychology of Women Quarterly 4.4 (1980): 492-507.

Studying younger women and those re-entering college, Bers finds that re-entering women tend to be more traditional with regard to the women's movement and ERA. If there are negative feelings toward the movement, there are negative feelings toward ERA. However, both groups share an egalitarian attitude towards women's issues. They do not equate all women's issues. They show stronger support for specific issues and policies than for a general re-ordering of society as would occur under the ERA.

4-2. Broder, Sherry and Beverly Wee. "Hawaii's Equal Rights Amendment: Its Impact on Athletic Opportunities and Competition for Women." University of Hawaii Law Review 2.1 (1979): 97-144.

Litigation under the equal protection clause of the Fourteenth Amendment has not been successful in ending sex discrimination in sports. The proposed Equal Rights Amendment could provide significant impetus for remedying sex discrimination in athletics. At present, not even separate but equal opportunities for female athletes are required and women are prohibited from playing on male teams even when no comparable female teams exist.

4-3. Foodin, Marilyn, et al. "Teaching about the ERA." Interracial Books for Children Bulletin 9.6 (1978): 3-7.

The objectives of the lessons are to broaden elementary school students' understanding of the need for the ERA, the importance of participation in the political process, and the need to support the ERA. The article includes a fact sheet on ERA and examples of sex discrimination.

4-4. Oglesby, Carole A. et al. "Women and Sport: From Myth to Reality." (1978) ED 152767.

This is a collection of essays on women, sport, and society. Historically, women have been denied sports training. The future of women in sports depends on the ERA and other civil rights legislation.

4-5.   Project on Equal Education Rights.   NOW Legal Defense and
       Education Fund.   Peer Perspective 4.2 (1978).

            This issue includes articles on the federal
       government's threat to cut off funds under Title IX and
       NOW's declaration of an emergency with regard to
       ratification of the ERA.

4-6.   Women's Rights Project.   (ACLU)   "Sports Packet."   (1979) ED
       166281.

            The Project presents a model legal case for defending
       a girl who wants to play soccer on her high school's all-
       male soccer team.   Included are descriptions of the
       impact of the equal protection clause and both state and
       federal ERAs.

4-7. "Action for Equity Marches on." Graduate Woman September-
        October (1980): 32-33.

4-8. "Information Social Studies Teachers Should Have." Social
        Science Record 12.3 (1975): 30-36.

4-9. McGuire, W. "NEA for ERA: the Final Push." Today's Education
        February-March 1981: 10+.

4-10. National Commission on the Observance of International Women's
        Year." Equal Rights Amendment, a Workshop Guide.
        Washington: GPO, 1977.

4-11. "No Unisex Sports." (Letter) Christian Science Monitor 7 May
        1979: 22.

4-12. Ryor, J. "The Equal Rights Amendment." (Editorial) Today's
        Education February-March 1978: 5.

4-13. Segal, P. N. "State Consitutional Equal Rights Provisions: Legal
        Tools for Achieving Sex Equity in Education." Journal of
        Educational Equity and Leadership 2.2 (1982): 85-99.

4-14. Sheely, A. C. and W. W. Wilen. "ERA Simulation." Social
        Studies 73.2 (1982): 52-56.

4-15. "Supreme Court Guts Title IX." On Campus with Women Spring
        1984: 1-4.

5 Family and Religion

5-1. Alexander, Elizabeth and Maureen Fielder. "Equal Rights Amendment and Abortion: Separate and Distinct." America 12 April 1980: 314-318.

The authors question whether the passage of the ERA would "lock abortion into the constitution". Most people who insist on linking the issues are opponents of the ERA, although "numerous Catholic organizations, political leaders, legal scholars and theologians reject the idea of a connection between these two issues." In 1977, the National Conference of Catholic Charities passed resolutions endorsing the Equal Rights Amendment and reaffirming its previous support for a Human Life Amendment. The Leadership Conference of Women Religious stated that "the issues around which the abortion debate rages are not the issues entailed in the Equal Rights Amendment....Persons who are strongly anti-abortion can be with full moral integrity just as strongly pro-ERA." The Canon Law Society of America, which does not support abortion, endorsed the ERA in 1979.

5-2. Becton, Betty Gordon and Betty Beld Moorhead. "What ERA Will Do for Family Law." Graduate Woman July-August 1979: 32-35.

This is a discussion of the impact of ERA on marriage, divorce, and marital property. The authors note that ERA is held responsible for changing social attitudes which are breaking down the rigid stereotypes in family life. "Passage of ERA would only continue the trend already well under way: to prohibit dictating different roles for men and women within the family on the basis of gender alone." (p. 32)

5-3. Conover, Pamela Johnston and Virginia Gray. Feminism and the New Right. New York: Praeger, 1983.

Over the last few years the ERA has become more closely linked with the abortion issue and the role of women in general. Both are seen as threats to the family and women's traditional role in the family. The opponents hold that the family and not the individual is the basic social unit. The assertion of women's individual rights and self-interest threatens this view. Operating on the state and local level the New Right prefers a grassroots structure. It is "primarily a counter movement engaged in a symbolic protest over the American family" and "it is linked only with the more recent conservative groups and not the older right." (p. 184-185)

5-4.   Divoky, E. "ERA Dead or Alive." Learning 6.9 (1978): 26-30.

The Equal Rights Amendment is opposed by Phyllis Schlafly's Eagle Forum and the Family Preservation League of Women.   Opponents "need to affirm traditional sex roles and to preserve a life in which gender is an overriding determiner." Often they are "working class people who see the traditional family as a refuge from an insecure and often frightening world in which change comes too fast." (p. 27)   ERA's supporters come from a broader social spectrum and include the National Coalition of American Nuns, the League of Women Voters, the Young Women's Christian Association, and the Republican National Committee.

5-5.   Fennelli, Maureen.   "Speak-out: 18 Women Tell Where They Stand on Some Simmering Issues of 1979." Working Woman April 1979: 54+.

These women speak about the women's movement, ERA, abortion, and gay rights.   All the women interviewed say the women's movement has had an effect on their lives.   They differ in their support of ERA, abortion and gay rights. Most are ambivalent about ERA but connect it to equal pay which they strongly support.

5-6.   Fiedler, Maureen.   "Bishops' ERA Position Avoids Equality Issue for Abortion Statement." National Catholic Reporter 8 June 1984: 30-32.

Disputing the link of ERA to federally funded abortion, Fiedler says this bogus issue "diverts public attention from the real issues: feminization of poverty, older women's need for fair social security insurance, discrimination, women's employment, homemakers' rights." An interdisciplinary committee of Bishops will investigate the link of ERA and abortion funding in response to the charge of the pro-life committee of the National Conference of Catholic Bishops. This committee is also concerned with the impact of ERA on "private education institutions, the tax exempt status of charitable and kindred organizations, religious exemptions in federal grant statutes, government aid programs, and other matters."

5-7. Foster, Marion G. "Eliminating Sex Discrimination in the Law."
      Social Casework 58.2 (1977): 67-76.

      Social workers have a responsibility to assist
      legislators in eliminating sex discrimination in the law as
      they understand the implications of equal rights
      amendments on family, child welfare, health care,
      corrections, and other social welfare concerns. Areas
      where social work experience is valuable in assisting
      legislators are: inequities in legal age of majority,
      employment conditions, domestic relations, child welfare,
      parole standards, rape laws, and inequality in Social
      Security.

5-8. Granberg, Donald. "Comparison of Members of Pro- and Anti-
      Abortion Organizations in Missouri." Social Biology
      28.3-4 (1981): 5-34.

      Granberg finds that pro-abortion organization
      members were better educated, urbanized and had fewer
      children. Anti-abortionists were predominantly Catholic,
      highly religious, committed to conservative politics and
      morals and were more militaristic. Pro-abortion groups
      favored ERA and were "more committed to free speech for
      social deviants." On women's issues other than ERA,
      anti-abortionists take pro-women's rights positions,
      though not as strongly as pro-abortionists.

5-9. Jones, Cathy J. "The Tender Years Doctrine: Survey and
      Analysis." Journal of Family Law 16.4 (1978): 695-738.

      Jones examines the preference of courts for awarding
      custody of minor children to their mothers, an historical
      development of the twentieth century. The courts use
      three tests in deciding custody: the best interests of the
      child doctrine, the tender years doctine, and the party
      without fault in the divorce action. The tender years
      doctrine presumes that young children are better placed
      with their mothers who are "best equipped to provide for
      the physical, emotional, and psychological needs of the
      child." (p. 696) The ERA if enacted would "make the
      tender years presumption unconsitutional."

5-10. Johnson, Sonia. "The Woman Who Talked Back to God and
      Didn't Get Zapped." Ms. November 1981: 51-54.

      Sonia Johnson was excommunicated by the Mormon
      Church in 1979 because of her work on behalf of the
      ERA. This article is an excerpt from her autobiography.
      Disturbed by the discussion of politics in Church, she
      began to study the ERA and to support it. Angered by

the trivialization of women's issues within the Church,
Johnson became radicalized. Struggling with the
Church's image of the maleness of God and the
preference for men, Johnson came to accept that God
would not zap women who question the myths which bind
them; and that men made God in their own image to
control women. Johnson chose to reorganize heaven, to
remember the Mother in Heaven. With this strength, she
continued her activity on behalf of ERA ratification.

5-11.   Kocol, Cleo Fellers. "Civil Disobedience at the Mormon Temple."
Humanist September-October 1981: 5-14.

Kocol and others chained themselves to the Mormon
Temple in Bellevue, Washington, to protest the "Mormon
menace." This is defined as the Church's use of its
wealth and influence in secular affairs. Her source is
the investigative reporting done by the Miami Herald on
the takeover by the Mormon Church of the Mormon's
women's organizations for political purposes and for
laundering of money to oppose ERA.

5-12.   Kurtz, Paul M. "State Equal Rights Amendments and Their
Impact on Domestic Relations Law." Family Law Quarterly
11 (Summer 1977): 101-150.

The author states that the area of domestic relations
law is "the most sexist in its traditional mandates,"--laws
involving alimony, divorce, child custody, and marriage.
It is in this area that the greatest controversy has arisen
over the impact of ERA. Kurtz is not convinced that the
ERA's absolute standard of sex neutrality is most
appropriate to family law.

5-13.   Marshall, Thelma E. "Women in the United States, 1976." Black
Scholar 9.8-9 (1978): 29-34.

Marshall traces the history of women's organized
attacks on discrimination from Seneca Falls to the current
feminist movement made up of well-educated middle class
women. "Minority group and working class women have
not yet been persuaded that their interests can best be
served by joining forces with NOW, WEAL and other
predominantly white, middle-class organizations." (p.
32-33) She urges passage of the Equal Rights
Amendment and a broader coalition of white and black
women.

5-14.   Mumford, Stephen D. "The Catholic Church and Social Justice
Issues: An Expose of Vatican Power in America."

Humanist 43.4 1983: 5-14.

Recent prominent theologians have attacked the Vatican and Catholic hierarchy for concerning themselves with power not with social justice. "This preoccupation with power has serious implications for non-Catholics as well, regarding some of the most sensitive and important social isses of the day. They include the Equal Rights Amendent, the environmental movement, legalized aboriton, family planning and population growth control, and illegal immigration control." (p. 5) ERA challenges the Church's authority and encourages women to seek activities other than childbearing and instilling Catholicism. It would lead Catholic religious orders to demand equality. "There would be unending challenges to the all-male leadership of the Church by these women." (p. 7) "I am certain that its [ERA] failure was the result of the success of the Roman Catholic Church's bold efforts to defeat it." (p. 12) "Phyllis Schlafly, a Catholic, and the 'organization' she headed, got more help from the Vatican and the Amercan bishops than most Americans can possibly imagine....The belief that the anti-ERA forces are also a grass-roots movement is ridiculous." (p. 14)

5-15.   Myricks, Noel. "The Equal Rights Amendment: Its Potential Impact on Family Life." Family Coordinator 26.4 (1977): 321-324.

There are many gender-preferred areas of family law which would have to be reviewed if the ERA is ratified: alimony, child support and custody, property ownership, and divorce. If alimony is available either husband or wife would have a claim to it, whereas, historically alimony supported the divorced wife. Child support would no longer be the primary responsibility of the man because of his sex, but both parents would be equally responsible. In most cases today, state courts award custody to mothers. Under ERA, judges would have to ignore gender-based presumptions in making awards. Legislators would have to either invalidate gender-based laws or extend the law to include both sexes.

5-16.   Tedin, Kent L. "Religious Preference and Pro/Anti Activism on the Equal Rights Amendment Issue." Pacific Sociological Review 21 (1978): 55-65.

The data in this study supports the journalistic speculation that anti-ERA activists belong to conservative denominations and that pro-ERA activists belong to liberal religious groups, at least in Texas. "The findings, in the case of the anti-ERA women, fit in well with the literature on the radical right. This literature often posits a causal link between membership in fundamentalist denominations and extreme political conservatism." (p. 64)

5-17.   Timberlake, Constance H.   "Black Women and the ERA."   Journal of Home Ecomonics 69.2 (1977): 37-39.

The author argues against the myth that black women do not support the ERA. The Fourteenth Amendment establishing equal protection does not take care of black women who continue to be excluded from "equality of human rights and equal employment opportunity." Lacking these rights, black women are relegated to low paying jobs in the service sector and are denied fringe benefits such as medical and life insurance, sick and maternity leave, and pensions. Often lacking education and training, black teenagers are harder hit. As disproportionate numbers of black women are heads of households, these patterns will continue unless ERA is ratified and the economic outlook for black women changes radically.

5-18.   Wohl, Lisa Cronin.   "A Mormon Connection? The Defeat of the ERA in Nevada."   Ms.   July 1977: 68-75.

Wohl asks why public opinion polls continue to show majority support for ERA and yet the ratification process is stalled?   She believes that the answer lies in who controls the state legislatures, specifically the Nevada state legislature. In 1977, James Gibson, the Senate Majority Leader, a Mormon convert and a chief leader in the Church of Nevada, caused the ERA to be defeated. Although only ten percent of Nevadans are Mormons, three of the most powerful committees in the Senate are headed by Mormons and the Church turned out in force to lobby against the ERA.

5-19.   Zezulin, L. S.   "Door-to-door with the Utah ERA project." (NOW's missionary project in Utah) New Directions for Women 11 (January-February 1982): 8+.

Working with NOW in Utah where the Mormon Church has organized a massive campaign against ERA, NOW confronts Mormons in their own backyards using their door-to-door tactics. Zezulin met with uninformed opposition. The Mormon Church had circulated anti-ERA pamphlets saying ERA would outlaw Social Security for housewives, make wives work outside the home, insist on federal day care for children, co-ed bathrooms, and gay rights.   Non-Mormons, who comprise 50 percent of Salt Lake City, overwhelmingly support ERA.

5-20.   Alda, Alan.   "The ERA: Why Men Care."   Ms.   July 1976: 48-50.

5-21.   Allen, S.   "Mormon Crackdown Under Attack."   Christian Century 5 March 1980: 259-261.   (Letters to the editor)

5-22.   "Alimony Without Sex Bias." (Editorial) Christian Science Monitor 7 March 1979: 24.

5-23.   Bers, T. H.   "Perceptions of Women's Roles Among Community College Women."   Psychology of Women Quarterly 4.4 (1980): 492-507.

5-24.   "Betty Friedan Is Back on the Barricades with a New Cause: Family."   People 16 November 1981: 147-150.

5-25.   Bombeck, E.   "What Do Women Want?   I'm Glad you Asked." McCalls May 1982: 166.

5-26.   "Catholic Women...."   Congressional Digest June-July 1977: 170-192.

5-27.   "Church and State."   New York Times 23 September 1979: D9.

5-28.   Conover, P. J. et al.   " 'Pro-Family' vs. 'Pro-Woman': Elite-Mass Linkages on Family Issues." (1982) ED 210219.

5-29.   Contreras, J.   "Selling ERA to Mormons."   Newsweek 13 July 1981: 26.

5-30.   Cook-Freeman, B.   "Women Against Women: The Rise of Antifeminism."   (1981) ED 196738.

5-31.   "Don't Hold Religion Against the Judge." (Letter) New York Times 14 January 1982: A24.

5-32.   "Dozens Back Feminist Facing Mormon Expulsion." (Sonia Johnson) New York Times 2 December 1982: I, 32.

5-33.   "8 in House Seek Mormon Judge's Ouster in Rights Amendment Case."   New York Times 7 December 1979: A23.

5-34.   Eisler, R.   "Thrusting Women Back Into Their 1900 Roles." Humanist March-April 1982: 46.

5-35.   "ERA Allies, Bishop Joust." (Bishop Norman F. McFarland vs. Feminists) National Catholic Reporter 3 November 1978: 1-3.

5-36.   "Equal Rights 'Missionaries' in Mormon Country."   New York

Times 15 May 1981: A23.

5-37. "Every Woman Needs a Room of Her own." Los Angeles Times 9 January 1983 :V, 5.

5-38. "Fear at Moody." (Bible Institute professor dismissed) Christian Century 31 October 1979: 1052.

5-39. Follis, A. B. "I'm a Full Time Homemaker With Three Children and I'm Spending a Year of My Life Campaigning for Equal Rights. Here's Why." Glamour March 1982: 144.

5-40. Freeman, J. "Prolifers: ERA Equals Abortion." In These Times 1 March 1984: 2.

5-41. Goetz, R. "Justifiable Exceptions to Religious Freedom?" Christian Century 16 March 1980: 38-40.

5-42. Goodman, V. "ERA; The New Face of Missionaries in Utah." New Directions for Women 10 July-August 1981: 1+

5-43. "Greek Orthodox Conference Shuns Equal Rights Stand." New York Times 6 July 1980: A14.

5-44. Howard, B. "Sonia Johnson and Mormon Political Power." Christian Century 6-13 February 1980: 126-127.

5-45. "In the Battle for the ERA, a Mormon Feminist Waits for the Balloon to Go Up." People 29 December-5 January 1981: 66-67.

5-46. "Idahoans Say Religion Won't Sway Judge on ERA." New York Times 26 December 1979: A20.

5-47. Jones, E. B. "ERA Voting: Labor Force Attachment, Marriage, and Religion." Journal of Legal Studies 12 (1983): 157-168.

5-48. "Judge Refuses to Drop Case on Rights Amendment." New York Times 19 August 1980: 8.

5-49. "The Judge Gave Up the Wrong Task." (Yielding his church job does not correct the appearance of bias) New York Times 29 January 1980: 18.

5-50. "Judge's Removal Sought in Suit Against ERA." New York Times 26 August 1979: 25.

5-51. Kaschak, E. "In Support of Responsible Advocacy: A Reply to Hatch." American Psychologist 38.8 (1983): 956-957.

5-52. Kanowitz, L. Equal Rights: The Male Stake. Albuquerque: U. of New Mexico P., 1981.

5-53.   Keating, K.   "ERA of Concern Now to the American Family."
        Better Homes and Gardens November 1978: 44.

5-54.   Keerdoja, E.   "Mormon Rebel Fights for ERA." (Sonia Johnson)
        Newsweek 6 October 1980: 16.

5-55.   Kelly, E.   "Equal Rights Amendment."   Social Studies 69.3
        (1978):   126-127.

5-56.   Leitz, J. A.   "Selling ERA Door-to-Door."   Ms.   February 1982:
        19.

5-57.   Macfarlane, E.   "Equal Rights Meets Its Martyr."   (Sonia
        Johnson) Macleans 21 January 1980: 37-38.

5-58.   McAlister, K.   "Sonia Johnson: ERA Fight."   Longest Revolution
        April 1982: 1.

5-59.   "Many Mormon Women Feel Torn Between Rights Plan and
        Church."   New York Times 26 November 1979: A1.

5-60.   Marty, M.   "Confusion Among the Faithful." (American churches
        and ERA) Saturday Review 25 June 1977: 10-11+.

5-61.   "Missouri Bishop Adds Support to ERA Cause." (Bishop Michael
        F.   McAuliffe) National Catholic Reporter 25 January
        1980: 3-5.

5-62.   "Mormon Church Excommunicates a Supporter of Rights
        Amendment."   (Sonia Johnson) New York Times 6
        December 1979: A26.

5-63.   Morgan, K. L.   "Equal Protection and Secular Humanism."
        Detroit Civil Liberties Fall 1980: 821-869.

5-64.   "Mormon Feminist Awaiting Verdict of her Church Trial." (Sonia
        Johnson) New York Times 3 December 1979: A18.

5-65.   "Mormon Feminist Faces Church Trial."   New York Times 27
        November 1979:   B11.

5-66.   "Mormon Judge Challenged on Rights Amendment Suit."   New
        York Times 24 September 1980: A7.

5-67.   "Mormon Temple Protest Leads to the Arrest of 19."   New York
        Times 18 November 1980: A10.

5-68.   "Mormonism and the Equal Rights Amendment Don't Mix."
        Christainity Today 4 January 1980: 63.

5-69.   "Mormons Eject ERA Activist." (Sonia Johnson) New York Times
        9 December 1979: A6.

5-70.   "NOW's Troubling Oppositon to a Mormon Judge." (Letter) New

York Times 13 January 1975, A25.

5-71.   O'Reilly, J.   "The Big-Time Players Behind the Small-Town Image." _Ms._ January 1983: 37-38.

5-72.   Papa, M. B.   "Catholics on ERA: Boost it, or Blast It?" _National Catholic Reporter_ 14 December 1979: 9-11.

5-73.   Papa, M. B.   "ERA: Catholics Debate Its [ERA] Effects on Family, Abortion, Divorce Laws." _National Catholic Reporter_ 28 December 1979: 16-18.

5-74.   Pippert, W. G.   "A President Rights-ly Divides the Word." (Biblical support for ERA) _Christianity Today_ 4 May 1979: 48.

5-75.   "Pro-ERA Proposal by Bishops' Unit Draws Praise in Ohio, Flak in Missouri." _National Catholic Reporter_ 28 April 1978: 36.

5-76.   Rush, M. H.   "Religion and ERA Battle in the Rockies; Broomfield, Colo." _Christian Century_ 23 February 1977: 164-165.

5-77.   "A Savage Misogyny." (Mormons excommunicate Johnson) _Time_ 17 December 1979: 80.

5-78.   Scott-Welch, M. and K. Mullins.   "Back Page: Is God for the ERA." _Ms._ May 1982: 102.

5-79.   "Selling the ERA to Mormons." _Newsweek_ 13 July 1981: 26.

5-80.   Shipps, J.   "Sonia Johnson, Mormonism and the Media." _Christian Century_ 2 January 1980: 5-6.

5-81.   "Sonia Johnson: In the Battle for the ERA." _People_ 29 January 1980; 66-68.

5-82.   Spring, B.   "What Would the ERA Mean for the Nation's Churches and Seminaries." _Christianity Today_ 21 October 1983: 32-33.

5-83.   Swidler, A.   "Catholics and the ERA." _Commonweal_ 10 September 1976: 585-589.

5-84.   Thomas, C. S. _Sex Discrimination in a Nutshell._ St Paul: West, 1982.

5-85.   Traxler, S. M. E.   "Nun Slams Anti-ERA Bishops: Passage of Amendment 'Moral Imperative'." _New Directions for Women_ 9 May-June 1980: 1+.

5-86.   "Twenty-three Catholic Bishops Call for ERA Ratification." _National Catholic Reporter_ 11 June 1982: 5.

5-87. U.S.   Congressional Caucus for Women's Issues. Equal Rights
       Amendment Briefing Paper. Washington: Caucus Staff,
       November, 1983.

5-88. Wales, M. J. "Irked by Sonia Johnson's ERA Crusade, Church
       Elders Throw the Book of Mormon at Her." People 3
       December 1979: 44-45.

5-89. Weathers, D. and M. Lord. "Can a Mormon Support the ERA?"
       (Case of Sonia Johnson) Newsweek 3 December 1979: 88.

5-90. Welch, M. S. and K. Mullins. "Is God for the ERA?"
       (Interviews with clergy) Ms. May 1982: 102.

5-91. "When It Rains, It Pours." (Sonia Johnson) New York Times 19
       January 1980: A26

5-92. White, R. "Mormons Vs. Us." Off Our Backs 12 February
       1982: 12-13.

5-93. "Why Homemakers Have to Have ERA." Christian Science
       Monitor 27 February 1979: 27.

5-94. Wohl, L. C. "Feminist Latter-Day Saint: Why Sonia Johnson
       Won't Give up on the ERA or the Mormon Church." Ms.
       March 1980: 39-40.

6 The Military

6-1. Cantarow, E. "Staying Out of the Trenches." New Republic 1 March 1980: 19-22.

Strange bedfellows aligned against President Carter's announcement on February 8, of his proposal to register women, along with men, for the draft. These include Phyllis Schlafly, the Rabbinical Council of America, the Union of Orthodox Jewish Congregations, the Women's International League for Peace and Freedom (which is against registration for anyone), the right wing Libertarians, the National Organization for Women and the National Women's Political Caucus. Bella Abzug argued against female registration and sacrifice until women enjoy more equal opportunity.

6-2. England, Mary Jane. "Political Briefing: Doctor Draft." Journal of the American Medical Women's Association 38.5 (1983): 138-139.

In a report issued in 1983, the U.S. General Accounting Office called for the medical draft to include men and women up to the age of forty-six because the next war will be, probably, a nuclear and a public health nightmare.

6-3. Goodman, Ellen. "Do You Feel a Draft?" Journal of the American Medical Women's Association 38.5 (1983): 139+.

Even without an ERA, the Department of Defense has moved to draft women,-all females in medical and health professions between the ages of 18 and 49. Though anti-ERA, the Pentagon is forced into this position as most health care workers are female.

6-4. Loewy, A. H. "Returned to the Pedestal." North Carolina Law Review 60.8 (1981): 87-101.

Rarely in the last decade has the Supreme Court upheld gender based classifications. Now, in its 1980 term, the Supreme Court in two decisions, one involving rape (Michael M.) and one exempting women from registration for the military draft (Rotsker), has once again supported protective legislation which will impair women's struggle for equal rights.

6-5.   "Draft or No Draft, an Eye on ERA." (Editorial) New York Times
       23 July 1980: A20.

6-6.   "ERA Must Bite the Bullet on Drafting of Women." Los Angeles
       Times 23 November 1983: II, 5.

6-7.   "For the Record." Washington Post 9 December 1983: 22.

6-8.   "Military Issue and the House Defeat of ERA." Los Angeles Times
       10 December 1983: II, 2.

6-9.   "Santucci Fears Draft of Women." New York Times 21 July 1980:
       B3.

6-10. "Sex in the Trenches." (Editorial) Wall Street Journal 30
       January 1980, 22.

6-11. "Thinking Things Over: Sex, Soldiers and the ERA." Wall
       Street Journal 19 March 1980: 24.

6-12. U.S. Department of Defense. America's Volunteers--A Report
       on the All-Volunteer Armed Services. Washington: GPO,
       1978.

6-13. U.S. Department of Defense. Use of Women in the Military.
       Washington: GPO, 1977.

6-14. "Women and the Draft." America 23 February 1980: 30.

7 Ratification Efforts

7-1. Arrington, Theodore S. and Patricia A. Kyle. "Equal Rights Amendment Activists in North Carolina." *Signs* 3.3 (1978): 666-680.

> The authors studied ERA activists in North Carolina; those who wrote letters to national newspapers, were public speakers, and were organizational leaders of women's groups. Arrington and Kyle investigated their political attitudes, personalities, socioeconomic status, religion, social cross-pressures, geography, and parental influences of the activists. They concluded that these activists were similar to the "traditional U.S. political elite."

7-2. Beyea, Patricia. "ERA's Last Mile: Women's Work." *Civil Liberties Review* July-August 1977: 45-49.

> Beyea, a staff member for the American Civil Liberties Union, questions the loss of momentum of ratification and reports on different strategies now underway; namely, aggressive political campaigns rather than low-key lobbying efforts.

7-3. Bird, Caroline. *What Women Want* (National Women's Conference, Houston Texas, November 1977). New York: Simon and Schuster, 1979.

> This book reports on the November, 1977 National Women's Conference. Numerous issues are considered as they relate to women. They include: arts and humanities, battered women, business, child abuse, child care, credit, disabled women, education, elective and appointive office, employment, the Equal Rights Amendment, health, homemaking, insurance, international affairs, media, minority and elderly women, offenders, rape, reproductive freedom, rural women, sexual preference, government statistics, welfare, and poverty. The history of each respective issue, analysis of present problems, and suggested actions which can be taken to solve them are outlined. (Modified abstract)

7-4. Cary, Eve and Kathleen Willert Peratis. *Women and the Law*. Skokie: National Textbook, 1977.

> Cary and Peratis explore why the legal protection offered by the Fourteenth Amendment and decisions

rendered by the Supreme Court have not eliminated sex discrimination. They believe that the defeat of the Amendment resulted from fear that protective labor legislation would end, that women would be forced into the labor market, forced to share half the burden of family and child support, forced to use unisex toilets, and be drafted. Historically, protective labor laws have kept women out of better paying jobs and are illegal under Title VII of the Civil Rights Act of 1964. If women were drafted, they would share with men the exemptions for hardship and childcare, and gain training and promotion.

7-5.   Crowell, S. "Four Days in Houston: Watershed for Women's Rights." Civil Rights Digest 10.2 (1978): 2-13.

At the National Women's Conference in Houston, Texas, 1977, the issues of women's rights became part of the national debate with women taking "their places in the general [political] alignment of Right and Left." The Conference was organized by the International Women's Year Commission which supported the ERA from its inception. The Conference adopted a National Plan of Action forwarded to President Carter.

7-6.   Cukor, Jane. "ERA is for Everyone." Graduate Woman January-February 1979: 11-13.

Reprinted from the Atlanta Journal and Constitution, Cukor (a middle-aged homemaker) writes why her family supports ERA. Citing the sex discrimination in the Georgia constitution and in the education of her daughter, she says that failure to ratify ERA is a recognition that equality of rights under the laws shall be abridged or denied women.

7-7.   D'Aulaire, Emily and Per Ola D'Aulaire. "Equal Rights Amendment: What's it All About?" Reader's Digest February 1977: 98-102.

This article summarizes the arguments both supporting and opposing the ratification of the ERA and clarifies what ERA will not do. It will not interfere with private rights, sex-segregated toilets or dormitories in federal institutions; encourage homosexual marriage; invalidate rape laws or states' rights.

7-8.   Denmark, Florence L. "Why the Equal Rights Amendment?" (1980): ED176151.

The ERA will end the artificial barriers between men and women which are applied legally, socially, and psychologically. This study argues that equal rights, equal protection, equal opportunity, and equal responsibility under the law do not require the same number of men and women in each role nor do they undermine the value of the family. ERA would establish individual choice rather than social prescription, allowing both men and women to benefit from the loosening of artificial sex-role definitions.

7-9. District of Columbia. Commission for Women. Report 1980-1982. Washington: The Commission, 1982.

This advocacy agency has built beneficial coalitions with many groups representing minority and ethnic groups including the National Association of Cuban American Women, the National Council of Negro Women, D.C., the National Forum of Hispanic Organizationa, the Organization of Black Activist Women, and others. "The Commission organization endorses the ERA and participates in all activities, including peaceful demonstrations and programs to help disseminate accurate information." (p. 15)

7-10. Dow, Phyllis A. "Sexual Equality, the ERA and the Court." New Mexico Law Review 13 Winter 1983: 53-97.

Having recognized the issue of sex inequality in Reed v. Reed (1971), the Supreme Court has ducked the issue in subsequent decisions excusing itself during the ERA ratification drive. Where it has spoken on sex discrimination, the Court refused to find sex discrimination as serious as race discrimination (Frontiero v. Richardson, (1973), and supported discriminatory schemes in Michael M. (1981, rape), and Rosker (1981, male military draft).

7-11. Follis, Anne Bowen. I'm Not a Women's Libber, but...and Other Confessions of a Christian Feminist. Nashville: Abingdon, 1981.

To her horror, Follis documents the right-wing ideologues who judge Christians by their political beliefs not their religious beliefs. Follis is active in the Homemakers Equal Rights Association. She reports her colleagues' misfortunes as they took public stands in favor of the ERA. Although she and her husband and child marched in 1978 in support of ERA, the opponents labeled the marchers as lesbians and radicals on national television news. She argues that both the old and new testaments have many examples of strong roles accorded women.

7-12.   Foss, Sonya K. "Equal Rights Amendment Controversy: Two Worlds in Conflict." Quarterly Journal of Speech 65.3 (1979): 275-288.

Foss asserts that the rhetoric generated by proponents and opponents of ERA creates "perceptions that--whether they correspond to reality or not--are more influential than the arguments presented to the public." (p. 275) For the proponents of ERA, there is a grass roots movement supporting women's rights to enter a world full of opportunity and they see their enemies as motivated out of self-interest and right-wing politics. Opponents to ERA see the home and the pedestal, not the world, as the proper sphere for women and the world full of horror were the ERA to be adopted. Opponents see themselves as "maintaining traditional social customs and institutions against the onslaught of reform." (p. 283)

7-13.   Ginsburg, Ruth Bader. "Let's Have ERA as A Signal." American Bar Associtaion Journal January 1977: 70-73.

Although the Supreme Court has taken a few remarkable steps when dealing with the validity of laws based on gender, the Court appears uncertain as to what constitutes sex discrimination and has shied away from doctrinal development. Ginsburg concludes that "the Equal Rights Amendment would provide the missing constitutional ingredient."

7-14.   Handburg, Roger and W. Lowery. "Women State Legislators and Support of the Equal Rights Amendment." Social Science Journal 17.1 (1980): 65-71.

Earlier studies of support for the ERA among traditional female populations in Texas and North Carolina show high correlation between support and educational achievement, youth, weak church affiliation, and Democratic party affiliation. This study of women state legislators' support for the ERA found two variables which appear to explain differing levels of support-- educational achievement and political party affiliation. The Democratic party legislators tend to be better educated and supporters of the ERA. As a group, women state legislators were overwhelmingly in favor of ERA.

7-15.   "Hollywood Mobilizes for the ERA." Ms. June 1978: 53-57+.

This is a picture essay of Hollywood stars with short statements by them in support of the Equal Rights Amendment. The stars included are: Candice Bergen, Marlo Thomas, Jean Stapleton, Alan Alda, Valerie Harper, and Norman Lear. Jean Stapleton says that as Edith Bunker she doesn't have equal rights and as Jean Stapleton she doesn't either.

7-16.   Howar, Barbara. "Waxy Yellow Buildup at the Houston Women's Conference." New York 5 December 1977: 39-42.

Meeting in Houston for the National Women's Conference, Howar reports on the excitement of 20,000 women convening. Addressed by prominent female supporters of the ERA, the Convention watched demonstrations of pro-family groups carrying signs calling for repentance and return to husbands and grapled with the divisive issues of abortion and homosexuality.

7-17.   Malinowski, Jamie. "Favorite Daughters 1980: Strategy for the ERA." USA Today November 1979: 16-9.

The author offers a strategy to move ERA ratification: pro-ERA candidates should compete in the presidential campaign of 1980. "I would field 25 or 30 women, each running in her own state as a Favorite Daughter candidate on a platform containing a single plank--ratification of the ERA." (p. 16) The purpose is not to defeat President Carter in the primary but to show that ERA's still a viable issue and its proponents well organized.

7-18.   Marshall, Thelma E. "Women in the United States, 1976." Black Scholar May-June 1978: 8-9, 29-34.

The author supports the ERA, applauds the achievements of the Women's Movement and looks foward to the development of broader coalition between middle class white organizations and the organizations representing ethnic minorities and working class women.

7-19.   Paul, M. "Campaign for Equality: From Seneca Falls, 1848, to ERA Deadline, 1982." Senior Scholastic 8 January 1982: 14-18.

Tracing the history of Seneca Falls (1848) through Suffrage to the present, 1982, where ERA is three states short for ratification and four states have voted to rescind; Paul asserts that 1982 is as decisive a year as

1828.

7-20.   President's Advisory Committee for Women.   Voices for Women:
        1980 Report of the President's Advisory Committee for
        Women.   Washington: GPO, 1980.

             This Committee is meeting for the ninth time since it
        was first established by President Kennedy in 1961 and
        chaired by Eleanor Roosevelt.   Commenting on the text of
        the ERA, committee member Erma Bombeck says that "no
        words have been so misunderstood since 'one size fits
        all'."   The Committee finds that the ERA is the single
        most critical step necessary to accelerate the progress for
        women and to guarantee that the institutions of the
        American government will truly provide equal justice for
        all. (p. 21)

7-21.   "A   Primer on the ERA; Back to Basics for this year's fight."
        Ms.   January 1977: 74-76.

             In a question and answer format, this article reviews
        some basic questions about ERA: why a constitutional
        amendment is needed; what it will do; what it will not
        do; its effect on bathrooms, the draft and abortion, and
        the legislative accomplishments in states with equal rights
        amendments.

7-22.   Segal, Phyllis N.   "Sexual Equality, the Equal Protection Clause,
        and the ERA.   Buffalo Law Review 33 (Winter 1984)
        85-147.

             Segal examines sex inequities which exist despite the
        Constitution's equal protection clause of the Fourteenth
        Amendment.   These are government policies "reflecting
        and reinforcing sexual inequality which are shielded from
        legal scrutiny because illicit intent can not be shown."
        Areas of inequity include Social Security law, pensions,
        employment policies, marriage and divorce laws, and
        welfare programs.   "In contast to the equal protection
        clause, the ERA would provide a constitutional principle
        directly targeted to securing equality of rights under law
        on account of sex." (p. 147)

7-23.   Slavin, Sarah, ed. "The Equal Rights Amendment: the Politics
        and Process of Ratification of the 27th Amendment to the
        U.S. Constitution."   (Symposium) Women and Politics
        Spring-Summer 1982: 1-86.

             In this collection of articles, Iva Deutchman and
        Sandra Prince-Embury write of the political thinking of

pro- and anti-ERA women ("Political Ideology of Pro- and anti-ERA Women"). In their small sample they find that religious orthodoxy and church attendance largely account for political ideology of anti-ERA women, more so than income and education. Opponents identified themselves as homemakers primarily unlike the proponents who identified themselves as professionals. The opponents resembled the religious right in orientation. Both groups were politically active and attended church or synagogue. Janet Boles' article "Systematic Factors Underlying Legislative Response to Woman Suffrage and the Equal Rights Amendment" sees similarities in the struggle for passage of the Nineteenth and Twenty-Seventh Amendments. Both grew out of broader social movements for women's rights. Each has economic, moral, and civil rights dimensions. Both were rejected by eight states in the deep south. Nonetheless, she finds it difficult to explain why suffrage became part of the Constitution within fifteen months of submission to the states while ERA fell three states short of ratification.

7-24. Strong, Frank R. "Contributions of ERA to Constitutional Exegesis." Georgia Law Review 14 (Spring 1980) 389-434.

The ERA raises two important constitutional law questions. Section One limits the U.S. or any state from denying equal rights on account of sex. Section Two gives the Congress power over intimate personal relations. Unhappy with the wording of Section Two, nonetheless, Strong calls for ratification of ERA as the way to end sex inequality.

7-25. Van Alstyne, William W. "Commentary: The Proposed 27th Amendment." Washington University Law Quarterly Winter 1979: 189-204.

Van Alstyne discusses the ERA in stylistic terms. He compares it to the first ten amendments as to language and style. He feels that the ERA has stalled because people have failed to understand that it is the nature of an amendment to be succinct and, therefore, find the ERA to be too ambiguous without every last detail spelled out.

7-26. Wohlenberg, Ernest H. "Correlates of Equal Rights Amendment Ratification." Social Science Quarterly 60.4 (1980): 676-84.

This is a study of state legislatures and their support for the ERA. The author finds that the more innovative legislatures, those which have ratified earlier suffrage amendments and those with more liberal religious and political views were significantly more likely to have ratified the ERA. Because they are more politically and religiously conservative it is unlikely that Mississippi, Alabama, Georgia, and Louisianna will ratify the ERA.

7-27.   Zussman, John. U. and S. M. Adix.   "Content and Conjecture in the Equal Rights Amendment in Utah."   Women's Studies International Forum 5 (1982):   475-486.

Public opinion on the ERA especially among its opponents is "based more certainly on conjecture, emotion and deference to authority than on objective knowledge of its content." (p. 475) Studying both the history of ERA in Utah and using an opinion survey, the authors say that until the Mormon Church announced its opposition to ERA, Church members were hardly unanimous in their opposition to ERA. The survey shows that support for the text of the Amendent was stronger than support for the Amendment. This leads the authors to believe that opposition to ERA in Utah is "not based on firm knowledge." (p. 484) The general public appears poorly informed on ERA." News reports often seem to emphasize the conflicts surrounding the ERA rather than its substance." (p. 485)

7-28. Adams, J. "Vows Last Push on the ERA." Guardian October 1981: 4.

7-29. Allen, G. "The ERA Won't Go Away - Nor Will Women." Humanist July-August 1978: 26-29.

7-30. "American Way; ERA." (Symposium) Redbook November 1979: 39.

7-31. Anderson, P. "Pennsylvania: ERA in Practice: How to Counter the Anti's Arguments." Ms. September 1978: 92.

7-32. "Archie Bunker's Loss is NOW's Gain." New York Times 1 April 1980: A16.

7-33. Arndt, R. "ERA--Yes: A Final Push in Key States." Nation's Cities Weekly 14 June 1982: 1+.

7-34. "As Women's Leaders Remap Their Strategy." U.S. News and World Report 6 July 1981: 54-55.

7-35. Askin, S. "Labor Adds its Voice to 'Pass ERA' Call." National Catholic Reporter 25 January 1980: 20.

7-36. Avner, J. S. "The Amendment Must Come Before, Not After, a Rights Act." Center Magazine November-December 1983: 14.

7-37. Barnett, M. W. "Why the Equal Rights Amendment?" Florida Bar Journal April 1977: 206-208.

7-38. Baron, A. "End of ERA? If You Think the Women's Movement is Dead, You'd Better Think Again." Politics Today November-December 1978: 6-7.

7-39. Bayh, B. "Question of Ratification of the Equal Rights Amendment--Pro." Congressional Digest 56.6-7 (1977): 170+.

7-40. "Betty Ford, Alan Alda in Forefront of Final Drive for ERA Ratification." Christian Science Monitor 12 June 1981: 6.

7-41. Bilgore, E. "ERA Stands for?" (What Girl Scouts think of ERA) American Girl July 1976: 18-19.

7-42. Block, J. L. "Some Thoughts on ERA." Good Housekeeping November 1979: 116-117.

7-43. Boulding, K. E. "The Ethic of Science and the ERA." Technology Review August-September 1978: 12.

7-44. Burnett, C. "Carol Burnett Talks up ERA." Working Woman December 1978: 88.

7-45. "Bush Favors Rights Plan." New York Times 19 September 1980:

B4.

7-46.   Buxenbaum, A. "Women Enter New Decade on the Offensive."
        Politcal Affairs March 1980: 17-22.

7-47.   Campbell, E. "Equality by Default: Women in Dual Roles."
        Intellect February 1978: 307-309.

7-48.   Carter, C. "What the ERA Means to Me." Essence March 1983:
        154.

7-49.   Carter, J. "Why Nice Women Should Speak Out for ERA."
        Redbook October 1977: 118.

7-50.   Carter, J. "Equal Rights Amendment." (Remarks, May 15, 1980,
        at a White House Briefing) Weekly Compilation of
        Presidential Documents 19 May 1980: 923-926.

7-51.   Carter, J. "Equal Rights Amendment." (Remarks June 18, 1980,
        at a Fundraising Dinner) Weekly Compilation of
        Presidential Documents 23 June 1980: 1122-1125.

7-52.   Carter, J. L. "Great American Bathroom Debate; Effects of the
        Equal Rights Amendment." Redbook April 1979: 58.

7-53.   Carter, J. L. "Look Who's for the ERA." (Support from men)
        Redbook September 1978: 67+.

7-54.   Carter, J. L. "The Reagan I Love." (Friendship and campaign
        for ERA with M. Reagan) Redbook March 1981: 21.

7-55.   Cassell, K. A. "Librarians, Politics, and the ERA" Wilson
        Library Bulletin December 1982: 292-294.

7-56.   Chapman, F. "Can 'Playboy' Buy Women's lib?" (Playboy
        Foundation and Chrisite Hefner's support of ERA)
        Majority Report 8.5 (July 22-August 4) 1980: 1+.

7-57.   Chassler, S. "Between the Lines." Redbook July 1981: 22.

7-58.   Clark, J. "NOW Reaches Homestretch on ERA." Gay News 12
        December 1981: 3.

7-59.   Cole, E. "Testimony of the American Nurses Association on the
        Equal Rights Amendment." Nebraska Nurse February
        1984: 4.

7-60.   Cole, S. C. "ERA: Why Should We Care?" Essence October
        1978: 143-144.

7-61.   Collins, L. "Black Feminists and the Equal Rights Amendment."
        Sepia October 1979: 18+.

7-62.   "Continuing Controversy Over the Women's Equal Rights

Amendment: Pro and Con." (Emerson, Ervin, Schlafly) _Congressional Digest_ 56.6-7 (1977): 162+.

7-63. "Countdown on the ERA." _Time_ 14 June 1982: 25.

7-64. Crow, E. "Inside Parents; Equal Rights Amendment." _Parents_ November 1979: 4.

7-65. "A Deadline Nears: Equal Rights Amendment Must be Ratified by June 30 or Die." _Senior Scholastic_ 8 January 1982: 16.

7-66. Douglas, C. A. and J. Kelly. "NOW National Conference."(October 6-9, 1978, Washington, DC) _Off Our Backs_ 8 (November 1978): 7+.

7-67. Dreifus, C. "Eleanor Smeal: What Made the Homemaker from Pittsburgh Move into the National Spotlight?" _Redbook_ April 1982: 60.

7-68. "Drive in Illinois for ERA Opened by Labor Leaders." _New York Times_ 28 April 1980: A16.

7-69. (Editorial) _Working Woman_ August 1981: 4.

7-70. Eisler, R. "Thrusting Women Back into Their 1900 Roles." _Humanist_ March-April 1982: 46-9.

7-71. Elder, J. L. "Article Five, Justicability, and Equal Rights Amendment." _Oklahoma Law Review_ 31.1 (1978): 63-109.

7-72. Emerson, T. I. and B. G. Clifton. "Should the ERA be Ratified." _Connecticut Bar Journal_ June 1981: 227-237.

7-73. England, M. J. "ERA: A Cliffhanger All the Way." _Journal of the American Medical Women's Association_ 37.3 (1982): 60-62.

7-74. "The Equal Rights Amendment: The Case for." _Christian Science Monitor_ 5 May 1980: 20.

7-75. "Equal Rights Amendment Invites Judicial Roulette." _Los Angeles Times_ 2 July 1983: II, 7.

7-76. "Equal Rights: One Last Try." _New York Times_ 13 June 1982: E9.

7-77. "Equal Rights Proponents, Facing Conservative Tide, Shift Strategy for '81." _New York Times_ 16 March 1981: A10.

7-78. "ERA at a Glance." _Congressional Digest_ 56.6-7 (1977): 163.

7-79. "ERA Backers, in a Final Drive, See a Chance for Surprise Victory." _Wall Street Journal_ 28 May 1982: 1.

7-80.   "ERA   Battle   Comes   Down   to   the   Wire."   Christian   Science
        Monitor 10 March 1982: 19.

7-81.   "ERA   Call to Action."   American Home July 1976: 24.

7-82.   "The   ERA   Countdown."   (Editorial)   New   York   Times   5   July
        1981: E14.

7-83.   "ERA   Countdown."   (Illinois   approaches   vote)   Time   12   June
        1978: 20.

7-84.   "ERA   Deadline."   Progressive September 1978: 6.

7-85.   "ERA   Deadline to Face Review by High Court; But Time Runs
        Out."   Wall Street Journal 26 January 1982: 6.

7-86.   "ERA: The Fight's Not Over."   Apartment Life November 1979:
        33.

7-87.   "ERA--the Gift of Equality for the Women and Men of America."
        House and Garden November 1979: 274.

7-88.   "ERA: Going to the Airways."   Ms.   March 1982: 21.

7-89.   "ERA--is it the American Way?"   Co-Ed November 1979: 6.

7-90.   "ERA   Matters."   (Editorial)   New York Times 27 June 1980: A30.

7-91.   "ERA   Needs   Black   Support,   Says   Activist   Flo   Kennedy."   Jet
        22 November 1979: 24.

7-92.   "ERA: A   Question   of   Human   Rights."   Working   Woman   August
        1980: 68.

7-93.   "ERA   Ratification;   Not   If,   but   When."   Christian   Science
        Monitor 13 October 1981: 73.

7-94.   "ERA   Stalled but Women Make Piecemeal Gains."   U.S. News
        and World Report 20 August 1979: 56.

7-95.   "ERA   Forces   Make   Plans   for   What   is   Likely   to   be   Final
        Ratification   Drive."   Christian   Science   Monitor   5   May
        1981: 14.

7-96.   "ERA   Forces Still on Offensive, but Battle Seems All but Lost;
        Florida May be Last Hope as Deadline Nears."   Christian
        Science Monitor 11 March 1982: 7.

7-97.   "ERA: Start from Scratch."   New Republic 29 July 1978: 8.

7-98.   "ERA: Then There Were Three."   (Surge of optimism) Newsweek
        7 March 1977: 22.

7-99.   "The   ERA: What it Will Do for You."   Mademoiselle November

1979:   130-131.

7-100.   "ERA: Where it Stands Now."   McCall's November 1979: 66-67.

7-101.   "ERA's   Advance   Impact."   Christian   Science   Monitor   30
         November 1979:   23.

7-102.   "Fight to Ratify."   Economist 23 April 1977: 48+.

7-103.   "Fight Waged in Illinois."   New York Times 5 June 1982: A8.

7-104.   "First Ladies Out Front; Views on Equal Rights Amendment."
         Time 5 December 1977: 25.

7-105.   "Florida House Votes, 65-53, for Rights Amendment."   New
         York Times 18 May 1979: A12.

7-106.   "Focus on ERA."   (Interview A. Fordham and S. D.   Ross)
         Mademoiselle July 1976: 122-123.

7-107.   Fox, C.   "Sex and the Single Amendment: ERA."   Macleans 31
         December 1979: 21-22.

7-108.   Fraker, S. et al.   "What Would the ERA Mean?"   Newsweek 31
         July 1978:   24.

7-109.   Freedman, M.   "Crucial Legal Import of ERA."   Nation   2
         September 1978:   166-167.

7-110.   Fry, Amelia R.   "The Two Searches for Alice Paul."   Frontiers
         7.1 (1983): 21-24.

7-111.   Gillespie, M. A.   "Getting Down: Equal Rights Amendment."
         (Editorial) Essence November 1979: 75.

7-112.   "Happy Anniversary, ERA."   (Editorial) New York Times 22
         March 1979:   A22.

7-113.   Hewson, M.   "Answers to ERA Questions."   McCall's June 1979:
         60.

7-114.   Hewson, M.   "ERA: The Deadline is Near."   McCall's February
         1982:   33-35.

7-115.   Hewson, M.   "A Singular Woman."   (Eleanor Smeal) McCall's
         March 1982:   2-3.

7-116.   Hilberman, E. and N. Russo.   "Mental Health and Equal Rights:
         The   Ethical   Challenge   for   Psychiatry."   Psychiatric
         Opinion 15.8 (1978): 11-19.

7-117.   Hill, C. J.   "Foremothers Beckon Us to Fight: ERA Deadline at
         Hand."   New Directions for Women May-June 1982: 1.

7-118. Hollyday, J. "Just Where is the ERA." (Editorial) Sojourners
        February 1982: 6.

7-119. Howard, E. "ERA: On the Move in Virginia." Ms. February
        1978: 19.

7-120. "Illinois Panel Approves Equal Rights Measure." New York
        Times 1 May 1980: A22.

7-121. "In the Running for the ERA." New York Times 3 September
        1979: B6.

7-122. Jaquitk, C. "National CLUW Backs May 16 ERA March."
        Militant 26 March 1976: 23.

7-123. "Jill Ruckelshaus, Republican Activist and Lecturer." Ms.
        October 1981: 94.

7-124. Johnson, S. "Zero Hour for the ERA." Working Woman
        February 1982: 36-37.

7-125. Karlan, S. E. "The Equal Rights Amendment." Women's Law
        Journal 68 (Winter 1982): 8-10.

7-126. Keerdoja, E. "LBJ's Daughter Stumps for ERA." (Lynda Bird
        Johnson Robb) Newsweek 17 December 1979: 15-16.

7-127. Kelber, M. "Don Edwards: A Powerful Ally in Congress." Ms.
        October 1978: 19.

7-128. Kennedy, J. B. "Why I Support the ERA." Ms. July 1976:
        51.

7-129. Kilpatrick, J. J. "ERA: Losing Battles, but Winning the War."
        Nation's Business October 1979: 15-16.

7-130. Kramer, S. and D. Wang. "Women Back ERA Abortion Gay
        Rights." Militant 2 December 1977: 3.

7-131. Lee, R. E. A Lawyer Looks at the Equal Rights Amendment.
        Provo: Brigham Young, 1980.

7-132. Lear, F. "Now is the Time to Get Organized." (Feminist
        movement) Nation 12 December 1981: 635-637.

7-133. Lewin, N. "Judgement Time for the ERA." New Republic 10
        February 1981: 8.

7-134. Lloyd, K. R. "Is it Ever Good Business to be Right?"
        (National Business Council for ERA) Working Woman May
        1980: 4.

7-135. Logsdon, L. and G. M. Barton. "ERA: The Issues."
        Psychiatric Opinion 15.8 (1978): 11-13.

7-136.   Marmor, J.   "The ERA and APA."   (Equal Rights Amendment
         and the American Psychiatric Association)   Psychiatric
         Opinion 15.8 (1978): 24-25.

7-137.   Martin, F. W.   "Columnist Erma Bombeck Campaigns for the
         ERA and That's No Laughing Matter."   People 12 May
         1980: 38-40.

7-138.   May, L. and J. Balzar.   "6 Democrats Vow to Back Abortion
         Rights and ERA."   Los Angeles Times 4 February 1984:
         I, 24.

7-139.   McGuire, W.   "NEA for ERA: The Final Push."   (Editorial)
         Today's Education February 1981: 10-12.

7-140.   "Men Behind the Women Behind the Rights Drive."   (Jimmy
         Carter and Gerald Ford) New York Times 19 January
         1982: A14.

7-141.   Mennear, A. S.   "Equal Rights Amendment: Where it Stands
         Today."   Good Housekeeping July 1976: 162.

7-142.   Mercer, M.   "ERA: What Would it Really Mean?"   McCall's July
         1976: 107.

7-143.   Meyer, K. and P. White.   "Equal Rights Amendment: Variations
         in State Support--A Preliminary Examination."   Southern
         Sociological Society 1978:   1330+.

7-144.   Miller, J.B.   "The Effects of Inequality on Psychology."
         Psychiatric Opinion August 1978: 29-32.

7-145.   Miller, J.   "ERA in Trouble."   Progressive May 1977: 8-9.

7-146.   "Mood at NOW Conference is Businesslike as ERA is Pushed."
         New York Times 8 October 1979: B11.

7-147.   Morgan, R.   "Alice Paul: Mother of the ERA."   Ms.   October
         1977: 112.

7-148.   Myers, L.   "A Giant Step Toward Equality?"   (Registration may
         brighten ERA prospects) New Republic 1 March 1980:
         15+.

7-149.   Myerson, B.   "How Would ERA Affect Your Life?"   Redbook
         April 1976:   66+.

7-150.   Nadelson, C. C.   "Major Issues in Mental Health."   Psychiatric
         Opinion 15.4 (1978): 8+.

7-151.   Nessel, J.   "It's Time the ERA Was Ratified."   (Teens should be
         active in the movement) Seventeen February 1982: 112.

7-152.   Newman, J.   "The ERA - What Would it Really Do?"   Woman's

Day 1 November 1979: 54+.

7-153. "No Alternative to ERA." (Editorial) New York Times 24 August 1983: 24.

7-154. "North Dakota Upholds Rights Vote." New York Times 8 March 1979: B5.

7-155. "Notes and Comments: Equal Rights Amendment." New Yorker 22 May 1978: 25-26.

7-156. "NOW Hear This." (Liz Carpenter on the ERA) New York Times 17 December 1979: C23.

7-157. "NOW Opens a Rights Amendment Drive in Illinois." New York Times 15 April 1980: A16.

7-158. "NOW Plans National Push for State ERA Ratification." Christian Science Monitor 23 October 1979: 10.

7-159. "NOW Recruits Volunteers to Work for ERA Passage." Christian Science Monitor 24 December 1981: 21.

7-160. Oliver, J. "Federal ERA Scoreboard." Ms. March 1976: 94.

7-161. "O'Neill Slates Vote on ERA in a Tiff Over Parlimentary Ploys." Washington Post 15 November 1983: A8.

7-162. Orrick, R. "Why ERA - Wrongly - Has 'em Scared." Working Woman January 1979: 17-18.

7-163. Orth, M. "Hot Political Issues of the 80's." Vogue April 1981: 290-1.

7-164. O'Shea, A. "Washington Watch; ERA." Working Woman March 1979: 82-3.

7-165. Papa, M. B. "Pivotal States Consider Amendment." National Catholic Reporter 21 December 1979: 19+.

7-166. "Parlimentary Push for ERA Wasn't so Shocking." Wall Street Journal 13 December 1983: 30.

7-167. Peratis, K. W. and S. D. Ross. "Primer on the ERA; Back to Basics for this Year's Fight." Ms. January 1977: 74-76.

7-168. Powell, D. M. "Countdown for ERA: The Equal Rights Amendment Hits the Home Stretch." Sojourners February 1982: 10-11.

7-169. "Psychologists Back Women, Chuck Magazine, Gear up for NHI." (ERA boycott of convention sites) Science 16 September 1977:1168.

7-170. "Ratification Facts and Figures." (Information on the states that have and have not ratified the Equal Rights Amendment) Graduate Woman March-April 1980: 12-13.

7-171. Rawalt, M. "The Equal Rights Amendment." Agenda 7.6 (1977): 11-13.

7-172. Reagan, M. and C. Douglas. "You Can be Anything You Want to be!" Redbook July 1976: 110-111.

7-173. "Reagan's Women." New Republic 28 October 1981: 5-6.

7-174. "Representative Don Edwards' ERA Allies Agree It's So Nice to Have a Man Around the House." People 3 July 1978: 30-31.

7-175. "Resolutions Approved by the AMWA [American Medical Women's Association] House of Delegates." Journal of the American Medical Women's Association 33 (April 1978): 180-182.

7-176. "Rights Amendment Debate Continues." New York Times 20 July 1980: 28.

7-177. "Rights Amendment Fight Nears Decision in Illinois." New York Times 10 May 1980: A8.

7-178. "Rights Amendment Issue Divides Psychiatrists." (According to many, the conflict has dramatized questions of sexist bias and insensitivity to women's needs that have long troubled their profession.) New York Times 8 May 1981: A28.

7-179. "Ripeness is All." New York Times 11 January 1982: A23.

7-180. Rockefeller, S. P. and H. W. Milliken. "The Equal Rights Amendment." (Editorial) Michigan Nurse January 1981: 4.

7-181. Roeske, N. C. "The American Psychiatric Association and the Equal Rights Amendment." Psychiatric Opinion 15.8 (1978): 10.

7-182. Rowes, B. "Polly Bergen (Who Doesn't) Thinks ERA Needs a Facelift." People 6 October 1980: 111-114.

7-183. Russo, N. F. and E. Hilberman. "ERA: Psychological, Social And Ethical Implications for Psychology." (1979): ED169397.

7-184. Sasscer, R. B. "Do Women in Puerto Rico Need the ERA?" Nuestro December 1980: 23-24.

7-185. Scalia, A., et al. "Legislative Vetoes and the ERA case."

(Amicus Curiae Briefs) American Bar Association Journal 68 March 1982: 362-363.

7-186.   Seligman, D.   "Bostonians." (ERA views of T.P. O'Neill) Fortune 8 September 1980: 33.

7-187.   Seligman, D.   "Fun and Frustration with Senator Hatch." Fortune 26 December 1983: 31-32.

7-188.   Seligman, D.   "Sex bias in the U.S. Code (as argument for passage of Equal Rights Amendment)." Fortune 3 November 1980: 41.

7-189.   "Senator Tsongas on the ERA." (Letter) Washington Post 7 June 1983:   A18.

7-190.   Shapiro, L.   "Battle for ERA." Mother Jones November 1977: 20+.

7-191.   "Showdown Over Equality." Senior Scholastic 9 March 1978: 10-11.

7-192.   Slonim, S.   "Janofsky [President of the American Bar Association] Plans Effort on Behalf of ERA. American Bar Association Journal 66 March 1980:   282.

7-193.   Sontag, S.   "Can Rights be Equal?" Vogue July 1976: 100-101.

7-194.   "South Carolina Proponents of Rights-Move Pessimistic." New York Times 28 January 1980: A14.

7-195.   "State of Emergency Declared!" (NOW says ERA is in state of emergency) Ms. June 1978: 24.

7-196.   Steinberg, L.   "The Long Haul for ERA." National Journal 31 December 1977: 2006-2008.

7-197.   "Still a Struggle for ERA." (Editorial) Christian Science Monitor 23 March 1979: 24.

7-198.   "A Term Paper by Two Harried Law Students Paves the Way to the Passing of ERA (Maybe)." People 30 October 1978: 41.

7-199.   "Test Marketing the Equal Rights Amendment." Graduate Woman May-June 1979: 7-8.

7-200.   Tiley, L. A.   "NOW Or Never for Women's Era." New Statesman 29 January 1982: 15.

7-201.   "A Troubled Decade for the ERA." Christian Science Monitor 22 March 1982: 5.

7-202.   "True to the GOP in Her Fashion." Newsweek 31 August 1981:

10.

7-203. "The Unratified ERA States are Also Right-to-Work." (Eleanor Smeal speech on Solidarity Day) American Federationist October 1981: 6-7.

7-204. Urbas, C. "My Side." (Maureen Reagan) Working Woman January 1981: 80.

7-205. Van Gelder, L. "ERA Heroines Won't Go Away." Ms. September 1982: 46-47.

7-206. "Virginia State Vote Sought on Rights Amendment." New York Times 6 February 1979: A12.

7-207. "Virginia's Female Legislators Rally Around Equality Issues." Christian Science Monitor 11 June 1981: 17.

7-208. "Voting on Equal Rights." New York Times 16 November 1983: A12.

7-209. Wall, J. M. "New Wisdom from Rosie the Riveter." (New approach needed for ERA, editorial)." Christian Century 4 March 1981: 219-220.

7-210. Wall, J. M. "The Real Issue for Women in Power." Christian Century 27 October 1982: 1067.

7-211. "We Like Limbo, Say ERA Allies." New York Times 31 January 1982: E7.

7-212. Weilder, M. "Alabama Women Push for ERA." Big Mama October 1976: 8.

7-213. "We've Been Asked: Is Time Running Out on ERA's Chances?" U.S. News and World Report 28 November 1977: 32.

7-214. Wexler, J. G. "Where Our Freedom Begins; ERA." Vogue November 1979: 76.

7-215. "What Does Equal Rights for Women Mean to You?" Parents Magazine June 1976: 12-13.

7-216. "What ERA Has Done for Me." Christian Science Monitor 22 February 1982: 23.

7-217. "What Would the ERA Mean?" Newsweek 31 July 1978: 24-25.

7-218. Wheeler, E. et al. "Guess Who's for the ERA." Ms. April 1977: 78-79.

7-219. "Who Needs ERA?" (Letter) Christian Science Monitor 27 April 1979: 26.

7-220. "Who's Afraid of Virginia's Senator? Not Liz, Who Comes Out Fighting for Women's Rights." People 18 February 1980: 30-31.

7-221. Williams, D. A. "Never Underestimate." (Democratic ERA plank) Newsweek 25 August 1980: 27.

7-222. Williams, M. S. "ERA: The Deadline is Near." McCall's February 1982: 31-33.

7-223. "Women's Rights Amendment: The Days Dwindle; ERA Backers Have One Year Left to Win Votes in Three More States." Christian Science Monitor 1 July 1981: 4.

8 Boycott, Extension, and Rescission

BOYCOTT

8-1. Cannon, Benjamin E. "Convention Boycotts Ruled Outside the Purview of the Sherman Act." Southern University Law Review Spring 1981: 263-270.

> Cannon comments on the dismissal of the Missouri suit against the National Organization of Women's (NOW's) boycott of non-ratified states. The circuit court found that NOW's action was politically motivated and therefore did not fall within the scope of the Sherman Act. Missouri argued that NOW's convention boycott had a significant economic impact on the state.

8-2. Larson, Charles U. "Boycott as a Persuasive Tactic in Attempting to Ratify ERA." (1982) ED 214224.

> This brief paper, presented at the annual meeting of the Southern Speech Association, argues that the Speech Communications Association's boycott of convention facilities in support of the ERA ratification has been ineffective. The author proposes that mail and phone campaigns aimed at legislators would be more effective.

8-3. Loutzenhiser, Janice. "ERA Boycott and the Sherman Act." American Business Law Journal Winter 1980: 507-519.

> The author discusses the legality of the use of boycotts by NOW and similar organizations as a lobbying tool for the ratification of ERA. She explains how boycotts are being used and the arguments of those who say such use is a violation of the Sherman Act. Her conclusion is that although there is no precedent which is directly comparable to the ERA situation, there are precedents showing "a strong Supreme Court policy against extending the Sherman Act to regulate activities of a political nature."

8-4. Medoff, Marshall. H. "Equal Rights Amendment: An Empirical Analysis." Economic Inquiry July 1980: 367-379.

> The purpose of this study was to test whether "discrimination against women in the marketplace is less in ratified states than in nonratified states." Medoff sees little to support the contention that states which have not ratified the ERA show greater sex discrimination.

8-5. "Aerial Display Presses Mormon Rights Drive." New York Times 6
      May 1980: D19.

8-6. "ALA Marches for ERA in Chicago Rally." American Libraries
      June 1980: 311.

8-7. "ALA Membership Vote Nixes ERA Stance." Library Journal 1
      May 1979: 996.

8-8. "Artists Donate Work for Lobbying Effort." New York Times 21
      November 1981: A13.

8-9. "As ERA Deadline Approaches: NOW Pins Efforts on New
      Strategies." Christian Science Monitor 20 October 1981:
      5.

8-10. "Backers of Equal Rights Hold Rallies in Four States." New
      York Times 7 June 1982: A12.

8-11. "The Big Question to Ask Your Shrink." Ms. May 1981: 25.

8-12. Borman, N. "One Hundred Thousand Dropouts of the 'Me
      Involvement' March on Capitol for Women's Rights." (NOW
      sponsered demonstration in Washington, D.C., July 9,
      1978, for ERA extention) Majority Report 22 July-August
      4, 1978: 1+.

8-13. "Both Carter and Kennedy Appear on Same Equal Rights
      Podium." (ERA fund-raising dinner) New York Times 19
      June 1980: A19.

8-14. "Boycotting for Amendment; Equal Rights Amendment."
      Christianity Today 10 February 1978: 30.

8-15. Braude, M. "Women Psychiatrists Triumph at American
      Psychiatric Association." Journal of American Medical
      Women's Association January 1981: 19-20.

8-16. "Briefing." (NOW campaign for ERA) New York Times 30 October
      1981: A9.

8-17. Buckley, W.F., Jr. "No Trespassing; Connecticut Directive to
      Professors Concerning Travel to States Which Have Not
      Ratified ERA." National Review 13 October 1978: 1303.

8-18. "Bush's Aid Sought on Rights Measure." (Fasters send
      telegram--aide says a meeting is unlikely) New York
      Times 15 June 1982: 13.

8-19. Campbell, D. "The OAH [Organization of American Historians],
      ERA and Feminism." Conference Group in Women's
      History Newsletter September 1978: 16-17.

8-20. "Chicago ERA Rally Sends Politicians, States a Warning."

Christian Science Monitor 12 May 1980: 9.

8-21. "Court Backs Missouri Boycott for Women's Rights." New York Times 29 March 1980: A6.

8-22. Crowl, J. "Association to Quit Chicago Over Rights Amendment." Chronicle of Higher Education 27 March 1978: 9.

8-23. Dillinger, W. "Another Route to the ERA." (Calling for special state conventions)." Newsweek 2 August 1982: 8.

8-24. "Don't Meet in Illinois in May; It Lacks ERA." (Women tell bishops) National Catholic Reporter 10 March 1978: 3.

8-25. "Dreams, Cats, and the ERA." (Psychiatrists' convention) Time 19 May 1980: 65.

8-26. Eisner, M.R. "ERA Boycott: Taking Our Gloves Off." Ms. May 1978: 80.

8-27. "Equal Rights Backers Demonstrate Near Convention." New York Times 15 July 1980: B6.

8-28. "Equal Rights Backers Hold Strategy Meeting in Illinois." New York Times 16 June 1982: A16.

8-29. "Equal Rights Backers March for Amendment." New York Times 23 August 1981: A14.

8-30. "Equal Rights Plan's Backers Vow to Defeat Opposition Legislators. New York Times 20 June 1980: A12.

8-31. "The ERA Boycott: Is it Working?" U.S. News and World Report 20 March 1978: 25.

8-32. "ERA Boycott Up for ALA Mail Vote; SLA Says Yes."(American Library Association and the Special Libraries Association) Library Journal 15 February 1979: 447-448.

8-33. "ERA Leaders Map Plans for Two Front Battle; Facing Deadline." (They need high court and state success) Christian Science Monitor 28 December 1981: 3.

8-34. "ERA March." National Review 4 August 1978: 939.

8-35. "The ERA Meet Me in St. Louis? Phooey!" (ERA Boycott Coalition). Majority Report 7-20 January 1978: 6.

8-36. "ERA Now?" (NOW boycott) Time 14 November 1977: 28.

8-37. "ERA Partners: Union-Feminist Ties Grow Firm in the Ratification Push." Wall Street Journal 15 December 1981: 1.

8-38. "ERA   Setback."   (Psychiatrists   withdraw   from   boycott commitment)" Time 7 April 1980: 62.

8-39. "ERA   Supporters." (Judge justifies boycott) Wall Street Journal 22 February 1979: 1.

8-40. "ERA vs. Chicago in '80--ALA Members to Decide in Mail Ballot." (American Library Association) Wilson Library Bulletin February 1979:   434-435.

8-41. "Feminists' Boycott; Support for the ERA."   Nation 26 November 1977:   548-549.

8-42. "Festive Rally for the ERA; Washington, D.C. March."   Time 24 July 1978:   18.

8-43. "Florida's ERA Vote: Convention Dollars at Stake, Too." Christian Science Monitor 4 April 1979: 7.

8-44. "Group to Distribute the Text of the Equal Rights Amendment." New York Times 30 November 1981: A13.

8-45. Guilford, C.   "Rally Supports ERA Fight."   Gay News 12 September 1981:   3.

8-46. Helary et al.   "ERA March for White Middle Class Hetero- sexuals."   (Chicago ERA march) Off Our Backs June 1980: 8+.

8-47. "Hunger Strikers in Illinois Taken to Hospital Twice."   New York Times 31 May 1982: A7.

8-48. "Hunger Strikers Rest a Day in Rights Amendment Vigil."   New York Times 29 May 1982: A9.

8-49. "Illinois Police Cut Chains of Rights Protestors."   New York Times 8 June 1982: A12.

8-50. "In Reversal, Historians Vote to Boycott States that Haven't Ratified ERA."   Chronicle of Higher Education 8 January 1979: 11.

8-51. "Judge Reaffirms his Order Approving NOW Boycott."   New York Times 22 March 1979: A16.

8-52. Karlan, S. E.   "Report on the Florida Capitol March and Rally for the Equal Rights Amendment."   Women's Law Journal Summer 1982: 90-91.

8-53. Koopmans, T.   "ERA and the Site of Annual Meetings."   (A Letter to the members of the American Economics Association) American Economic Review June 1978: 493-496.

8-54. "Lobbyists Press Illinois Capital on Rights Plan: Women Divide Rotunda as Fasting Continues." New York Times 20 June 1982: A19.

8-55. Lootens, T. "ERA Vigil--Threat to ...? Off Our Backs June 1984: 5-6.

8-56. McDonald, M. S. "ERA Boycott." McCall's August 1978: 67.

8-57. McKenna, C. "ERA Petitioners Arrested." New Directions for Women March-April 1982: 1+.

8-58. "Marketing Blitz to Sell Equal Rights." Business Week 19 April 1976: 146.

8-59. "Medical Librarians and ERA: Dade and Atlanta Boycott." Library Journal 15 March 1978: 603-604.

8-60. Miller, E. and M. Miller. "ERA D-day 1978; the ERA National March: the Viewpoint of Two Participants." Sister Advocate 25 July 1978: 6-7.

8-61. Nelson, M. "Running Away From Home." (Editorial on ERA boycott of Chicago) Wilson Library Bulletin March 1979: 484.

8-62. "New Track on ERA." New York Times 3 July 1982: A19.

8-63. "No ERA? No AAAS." (American Association for the Advancement of Science boycotts) Change May 1978: 41.

8-64. "NOW Meeting Turns to Raising Funds for Rights Proposal." New York Times 12 October 1981: A20.

8-65. "NOW Picks Illinois as Main Target." (Drive for Rights Amendment) New York Times 9 October 1979: A16.

8-66. "NOW to Switch Tactics on ERA." New York Times 14 October 1979: E7.

8-67. "NOW's Chief Barred from Carter Parley." (Group conducts a protest outside White House as other women confer on rights effort) New York Times 14 December 1979: B10.

8-68. "NOW's Funds Soar in Amendment Bid." New York Times 20 May 1982: A19.

8-69. "On to Washington!" (Indian march and ERA activities) Newsweek 24 July 1978: 34-35.

8-70. "One Million Dollar Radio Drive Begun for Rights Plan." New York Times 28 October 1981: A9.

8-71. "Party; ERA Fund Raising." People 1 May 1978: 44-46.

8-72. "Prayer, Walk Push ERA." National Catholic Reporter 23 May 1980: 6.

8-73. "Psychiatrists Shift Convention." New York Times 10 May 1980: 8.

8-74. "Psychiatrists to ERA: Never Mind." Science News 5 July 1980: 6.

8-75. "Psychologists Back Women, Chuck Magazine, Gear Up for NHI." Science September 1977: 1168.

8-76. "Rallies in Three Other States." New York Times 7 June 1982: A12.

8-77. "Reagan Criticized at a Rights Rally." (Betty Ford and Helen Milliken among speakers in Capital urging an amendment) New York Times 13 October 1981: 12.

8-78. "Rights Backers Stage a Protest in Detroit Park." (Republican platform ERA protest) New York Times 15 July 1980: B6.

8-79. "Rights Supporters Stop Illinois House Action." New York Times 17 June 1982: A24.

8-80. Ruderman, G. "As Time Runs Out for the ERA, Eight Women Stage an Ordeal by Hunger in Illinois." People 28 June 1982: 93-94.

8-81. "Shrinks Lobotomize ERA." Mother Jones July 1980: 10.

8-82. "Six Thousand Rally at the Virginia Capitol in Drive for Equal Rights Measure." New York Times 14 January 1980: A12.

8-83. "SLA Joins Boycott." (Special Libraries Association) Wilson Library Bulletin February 1979: 436.

8-84. "Spotlight on Returning to Chicago." (American Libraries Association's Midwinter Conference and ERA) American Libraries February 1979: 54-55.

8-85. "States Refusing to Ratify ERA Could be Boycotted by Directors." Variety 28 October 1981: 2-3.

8-86. "Steelworkers Shift Site of '80 Talk for ERA." New York Times 13 May 1979: A26.

8-87. "Thousands at a Rally in Chicago Back Equal Rights Amendment." New York Times 11 May 1980: A22.

8-88. "Twelve Illinois Women Jailed for Equal Rights Protest." New York Times 3 July 1982: A7.

8-89. "Twilight of the ERA." (Women rally as time runs out) Time 13

July 1981: 17.

8-90.   Van Til, W.   "Convention Sites and the ERA."   Phi Delta Kappan
June 1978: 713-714.

8-91.   Walsh, J.   "78 AAAS Meeting Moved from Chicago to Houston;
ERA Support."(American Association for the Advancement
of Science) Science 3 March 1978: 954.

8-92.   Wilson, J.H.   "Report from Joan Hoff Wilson." (Special report on
the American History Association's refusal to endorse the
national boycott of non-ERA states) Conference Groups in
Women's History Newsletter September 1978: 1-3.

8-93.   "Women Give Up Careers to Crusade for Equality."   New York
Times 8 November 1981: A20.

8-94.   "Women Rally for Rights in the Illinois Capitol."   New York
Times 4 June 1982: A14.

8-95.   "Women Relent on Boycott."   New York Times 2 August 1982:
A10.

8-96.   "Women Say They'll End Fast but Not Rights Fight."   New York
Times 24 June 1982: A14.

8-97.   "Women Try New Paths on Rights."   New York Times 14 August
1983: E5.

8-98.   "Women's Organization Assails 101 as Equal Rights Defectors."
(NOW vs. anti-ERA Democratic state legislators) New
York Times 27 June 1982: A18.

EXTENSION AND RESCISSION

8-99.   Almond, Michael A. and Ronald D. Rotunda.   "Running Out of
Time: Can the ERA be Saved?"   American Bar Association
Journal October 1978: 1504-1509.

While not opposing the ERA on its merits, Almond
finds the deadline extension to be "a subversion of our
constitutional process."   Rotunda disagrees and argues
that case law shows that Congress and "not the president
and not the Supreme Court ... is the ultimate guarantor
of many of our liberties;" and it can extend the deadline
for ratification.

8-100.   Berlow, Alan.   "Constitutional Law Experts Disagree Over
Extension of ERA Approval Deadline."   Congressional
Quarterly Weekly Report 26 November 1977: 2493-2496.

Berlow reviews the areas of disagreement: "whether
the constitution gives Congress the right to extend
ratification; whether extension would require a simple
majority vote by the House and Senate or a two-thirds
vote; and whether states that have already ratified the
ERA can rescind their approval."

8-101.   Carroll, John F.   "Rescission of Ratification: Extension of
Ratification Period."   Akron Law Review Summer 1982:
151-161.

The District Court in Idaho ruled in Freeman (1981)
that once Congress has set a reasonable time limit for the
states to ratify an amendment, it can not change the time
period.   The District Court ruled that since an extension
is not legal, Idaho has the right to rescind its prior
ratification.

8-102.   "Equal Rights Amendment and Article V - Framework for
Analysis of the Extension and Rescission Issues."
(Comments) University of Pennsylvania Law Review 127.1
(1978): 494-532.

This article studies the issues of extension of the
period for ratification and state rescission of ratification,
in light of the provisions of Article V of the
Constitution.   Nothing is found in Article V which would
prevent Congress from accepting efforts at both
extension and rescission.   Nor is the likelihood of
Supreme Court intervention seen no matter what decision
Congress arrives at.

8-103.   Freedman, Samuel S. and Patricia J. Naughton.   ERA, May a
State Change Its Vote?"   Detroit: Wayne State, 1978.

There is no history of rescission either in The Federalist or in state constitutional debates. Article V of the Constitution speaks solely of ratification and contains no provision for rejection. There is no relevant congressional statute. This prevents amendments from being subject to the changing climate of public opinion. Contrary to the opinions expressed by former Senator Sam Ervin (D-NC) on the legality of rescission, state actions are "simply not the same thing and are subject to different procedures." (p. 13.)

8-104.   Ginsburg, Ruth Bader. "Ratification of the Equal Rights Amendment--A Question of Time." Texas Law Review 57.6 (1979): 919-945.

Ginsburg answers the questions surrounding the effort to extend the deadline for ratification of the ERA. Based on her study of precedent and constitutional law, she finds that such a measure would need only a simple majority of both houses of Congress and would not require the president's signature. On the question of rescission, she feels this matter should be better left unanswered until such a time as it is key.

8-105.   Griffe, E. "ERA : How Extension was Won." Graduate Woman Winter 1978-9: 8+.

The extension victory showed that women have muscle. Under the leadership of Representatives Elizabeth Holtzman (D. NY) and Don Edwards (D. CA) the drive for extension in the House was successful. Representatives of religious, civil rights, public interest groups, and women's organizations met with labor lobbyists, White House and Congressional staffers and planned strategy. The women then applied their expertise to the Senate.

8-106.   Kanowitz, Leo and M. Klinger. "Can a State Rescind Its Equal Rights Amendment Ratification?" Hastings Law Journal 28.4 (1977): 979-1009.

With regard to rescission of earlier ratification by state legislatures, the authors consider two questions: 1) which branch of the federal government is to decide whether rescinded raification should be included in the first count--the Supreme Court or the Congress; and 2) how should the substantive issue be resolved on its merits? They argue that the Supreme Court is to decide and it should find that rescission is null and void. Should the Court decide that Congress should determine the merits of rescission, Congress should adhere to its past practice of counting only earlier ratifications and ignoring subsequent rescissions.

8-107.   Miller, Maxwell A.   "The ERA Ratification Game: Changing the Rules at Halftime." Student Lawyer 8 (1980): 9-11.

Miller sees the ERA extension as a violation of fundamental fairness and that due process must be defended if an individual's liberties are to survive. He supports the law suits brought by Arizona and Indiana which are supported by the Mountain States Legal Foundation to validate the states' rescission of the ERA.

8-108.   Millet, Thomas. "The Supreme Court, Political Questions, and Article V-A Case for Judicial Restraint." Santa Clara Law Review 23 (1983): 745-768.

At no time has the Supreme Court entered into the constitutional amendment process. Were it to decide on the ERA extension, the Court would be violating the separation of powers. The Supreme Court declined to hear the Carmen v. Idaho (1982) case which raised questions about state rescission and congressional extension of ratification before 1982. The Court found the case moot, thus, refusing to enter into the political controversy.

8-109.   O'Brein, Francis William.   "The Equal Rights Amendment: Is There a Life Hereafter?" Oklahoma Law Review 35 (1982): 73-85.

O'Brein reviews the history of court cases involving amendments in light of the recent Idaho v. Freeman (1981) case on rescission of the ERA currently before the Supreme Court. "Common sense demands 38 fresh ratifications for a fresh amendment" under an extended deadline." (p. 83)

8-110.   Rees,   Grover.   "Throwing   Away   the   Key--the Unconstitutionality of the Equal Rights Amendment Extension." Texas Law Review 58.5 (1980): 875-932.

Rees's concern is for the integrity of the amending process. He opposes extension because it violates the principle of amending the Constitution by consensus and because the Amendment specifies a time period for ratification. Therefore, the state legislatures which have ratified the ERA are not bound by that ratification after 1979 when clearly a consensus (38 states) had not been reached.

8-111.   Rees, Grover.   "When the Voting Should Have Stopped." National Review 18 August 1978: 1010-1013.

Rees considers the issues surrounding the extension of the time limit for the ratification of ERA. He looks at precedents regarding rescission, and the arguments for and against extension with and without rescission. He concludes that extending the time limit for ERA would set a poor precedent of allowing Congress unchecked power in amending the Constitution.

8-112. Vieira, Norman. "The Equal Rights Amendment; Rescission, Extension and Justiciability." Southern Illinois University Law Journal Winter 1981: 1-20.

He discusses the different time limits set for ratification of earlier amendments. It is a difficult question to extend the ratification deadline of the ERA because the seven year time limit for ratification was incorporated within the Amendment in the same joint resolution.

8-113. Witter, Jean. "Extending Ratification Time for the Equal Rights Amendment: Constitutionality of Time Limitations in the Federal Amending Process." Women's Rights Law Reporter Summer 1978: 209-225.

Witter explores the questions surrounding the extension of the time limit on the ratification of ERA. She concentrates on the history and legality of setting a time limit for the ratification of an amendment. She concludes that the Equal Rights Amendment, if ratified due to the extended time allowed, should be upheld.

8-114.   Benck,   E.   A.,   Jr.   "Standing   for   State   and   Federal
          Legislators."   Santa   Clara   Law   Review   Summer   1983:
          811-846.

8-115.   Berlow,   A.   "ERA   Extension   Wins   in   House   on   233-189   Vote."
          Congressional   Quarterly   Weekly   Report   19   August   1978:
          2214-2215.

8-116.   Berlow,   A.   "Rescission   Defeated: House   Committee   Approves
          Three   Year   ERA   Extension."   Congressional   Quarterly
          Weekly   Report   22   July   1978:   1852-1853.

8-117.   Berlow,   A.   "Senate   Clears   Extension   of   ERA   Deadline."
          Congressional   Quarterly   Weekly   Report   7   October   1978:
          2724.

8-118.   Berns,   W.   "Breaking   the   Rules: Congress   and   the   ERA."
          Atlantic   May   1979:   66-67.

8-119.   "Bill   to   Rescind   ERA   Passed   in   South   Dakota."   New   York
          Times   2   March   1979:   A10.

8-120.   Buchanan,   C.   "Extension   Asked   for   Equal   Rights   Amendment."
          Congressional   Quarterly   Weekly   Report   5   November   1977:
          2369-2370.

8-121.   Dworkin,   S.   "ERA--Phase   II;   We'll   Do   it   Again   Until   They   Get
          it   Right."   Ms.   April   1979:   66-67.

8-122.   "ERA   and   the   Question   of   Rescission."   Congressional   Digest
          June   1977:   168-171.

8-124.   "ERA   Bid   Moves   into   Overtime: As   Deadline   Extension   Takes
          Effect,   Opponent   Schlafly   Claims   Victory,   Backers   Await
          Vote   in   Florida."   Christian   Science   Monitor   23   March
          1979:   3.

8-125.   "ERA,   But   Not   this   Way."   (Editorial)   Washington   Post   15
          November   1983:   A14.

8-126.   "ERA   Deadline."   (Extended)   Progressive   September   1978:   6.

8-127.   "ERA   Runs   into   a   Roadblock."   Time   26   February   1979:   19.

8-128.   "ERA: Start   from   Scratch."   (Extending   ratification   deadline)
          New   Republic   29   July   1978:   8-9.

8-129.   "ERA   Troubles."   (Backers   want   more   time)   Time   27   March   1978:
          16.

8-130.   "Extension   of   ERA--the   Long   and   Short   of   it."   Nation's
          Business   June   1978:   22-23.

8-131.   "A   Festive   Rally   for   the   ERA."   (Lobby   to   extend   ratification deadline) Time 24 July 1978: 18.

8-132.   Goodman, W. "American Rules; ERA Extension." New Leader
         25 September 1978: 14.

8-133.   Holtzman, E. "More Time to Ratify ERA?" U.S. News and
         World Report 14 August 1978: 29-30.

8-134.   Hoover, E. "Winners Extension of ERA Ratification Deadline."
         People 30 October 1978: 41.

8-135.   MacLean, J. "Women Fight Back." Progressive February 1979:
         38-40.

8-136.   "New ERA; Senate Vote to Extend the ERA's Ratification
         Deadline." Newsweek 16 October 1978: 38.

8-137.   "No Time Limit on Equality." Graduate Woman September-
         October 1979: 8-10.

8-138.   "NOW Asks High Court to Reverse Idaho Judge's Equal Rights
         Ruling." New York Times 9 January 1982: 9.

8-139.   "NOW Will Appeal Idaho Ruling to Supreme Court." New York
         Times 24 December 1981: 11.

8-140.   Schliessmann, M. R. "Fantasy Theme Analysis: An Explanation
         and Application to the Rhetoric of the Equal Rights
         Amendment Extension Controversy." DAI 43 (1982):
         587A. University of Kansas.

8-141.   Shrum, R. "ERA Extension: All's Fair." New Times 13
         November 1978:

8-142.   Smeal, E. "The ERA Changing the Rules in Mid-Game."
         Majority Report 21 January/3 February 1978: 1+.

8-143.   Steinberg, L. "The Long Haul for ERA - and Now Division in
         the Ranks: Supporters of the Equal Rights Amendment
         are Divided over the Wisdom of Seeking an Extension of
         the Ratification Deadline." National Journal 31 December
         1977: 2006-8.

8-144.   Thom, M. "A New Lease on Life for the ERA?." (Case for
         extension) Ms. May 1978:56.

8-145.   U.S. House. Committee on the Judiciary. Proposed Equal
         Rights Amendment Extension: Report. H.J. Res. 638.
         Washington: GPO, 1978.

8-146.   U.S. Senate. Committee on the Judiciary. Subcommittee on the
         Constitution. Equal Rights Amendment Extension:
         Hearings. S.J. Res. 134. Washington: GPO, 1979.

8-147. U.S. Congress. Joint Resolution Extending the Deadline for the Ratification of the Equal Rights Amendment. H.J. 638. Washington: GPO, 1978.

8-148. "U.S. Asks Court to Block Ruling on ERA Extension." Christian Science Monitor 15 January 1982: 2.

8-149. "U.S. Judge Rebuffs ERA Extension." Christian Science Monitor 24 December 1981: 2.

8-150. "U.S. Judge Upholds Original Deadline on Equal Rights." New York Times 24 December 1981: A1.

8-151. "U.S. to Appeal Ruling that Upset Longer Deadline on Equal Rights." New York Times 5 January 1982: A1.

8-152. "U.S. to Appeal a Decision Nullifying ERA Extension." Christian Science Monitor 6 January 1982: 2.

8-153. "Winning Measure Extending Term for Ratification of the ERA; Work of S.R. Weddington." New Yorker 23 October 1978: 32-3.

9 Defeat

9-1. Arrington, Theodore S. and Patricia A. Kyle. "Equal Rights
      Amendment Activists in North Carolina." Signs 3.3
      (1978): 666-680.

> They find that activists supporting the ERA tend to
> have the characteristics of typical activists, whereas
> anti-ERA women are generally not similar to the usual
> political elite in their actions. Most are motivated by this
> one issue and are often mobilized by ministers opposed to
> the ERA.

9-2. Boles, Janet K. The Politics of the Equal Rights Amendment.
      New York: Longman, 1979.

> Even though the media favored the passage of ERA
> by featuring the arguments of the opponents alongside
> those of the proponents; the message of the anti-ERA,
> especially Schlafly as the undisputed spokesperson of the
> opposition, received wider publicity. The absence of
> wholehearted support from elected officials also served
> the opponents. The omission of support of the ERA in
> the Republican Party platform and President Reagan's
> refusal to endorse the ERA further legitimized the
> opposition and diminished chances for success.

9-3. Burris, Val. "Who Opposed the ERA? An Analysis of the Social
      Bases of Antifeminism." Social Science Quarterly 66.4
      (1983): 305-317.

> Burris identifies three factors in explaining the
> failure of the ERA to be ratified: "1) the low support for
> the amendment among politically influential groups; 2) the
> uneven geographic distribution of ERA support; and 3)
> the association between ERA opposition and a broader
> right-wing backlash." (p. 305) Reviewing the National
> Election Study, she finds no significant difference
> between male and female support for the ERA; black and
> minority support was stronger than white; no strong age
> group distinction; women with advanced degrees
> supported ERA, men did not. Men with high school
> educations were the strongest supporters. Women with
> larger incomes supported ERA: men did not. With the
> exception of high support among Jews and low support
> among Mormons "religious affiliation was not consistently
> related to ERA attitudes." (p. 310) Rural residence was
> strongly related to ERA opposition. ERA supporters
> were concentrated on the east and west coasts:
> opponents in south and central states.

9-4.   Caulfield,   Peter   James.   "Rhetoric   and   the   Equal   Rights
       Amendment: Contemporary   Means   of   Persuasion."   DAI
       45 (1984): 2507A (University of Michigan).

       Examining a decade's worth of writing on the ERA in
       organizational   newsletters   newspapers   and   magazines:
       Caulfield finds that the ERA was the most visible and the
       most threatening symbol of feminism.   Opponents of ERA
       recognized   this   threat   and   exacerbated   it   through
       persuasive   emotional   appeals.   Pro-ERA   groups
       underestimated this threat or chose to ignore it. Instead
       they argued on the basis of rational economic arguments
       which did not properly respond to this fear.

9-5.   Conover, Pamela Johnston and Virginia Gray.   Feminism and the
       New Right.   Praegar, 1983.

       The ERA was defeated because it was seen as
       advocating the rights of the individual in preference to
       the rights of the family--the most basic unit of society.
       The New Right believes women's role in the family to be
       defined by reproduction and childrearing functions. This
       view sees a natural division of activities between male,
       public and extra-familial jobs and the private, intro-
       familial roles performed by the woman.   As with the
       abortion debate, the injection of religion and morality into
       the equal rights debate appears to be new.

9-6.   Conover,   Pamela   J.,   et   al.   "Single-Issue   Voting: Elite-Mass
       Linkages."   Political Behavior 4.4 (1982): 309-331.

       They identify the ERA and abortion as examples of
       single issue politics and suggest that political activists
       may be cuing people into a pattern of single-issue voting
       and   making   the   battles   over   these   issues   especially
       intense.

9-7.   Ehrenreich, Barbara.   The Hearts of Men: American Dreams and
       the Flight from Commitment.   New York: Doubleday,
       1983.

       A legitimate fear of the New Right is men's flight
       from commitment.   Women who support Phyllis Schlafly
       want to preserve men's responsibility to support them
       and their children, since they believe that poverty awaits
       them should their husbands not provide.   It was the
       women's movement's failure to recognize this legitimate
       fear of many wives which helped to defeat the ERA.

9-8.   Eisenstein, Zillah R.   "Some Thoughts on the Patriarchal State and the Defeat of the ERA."   Journal of Sociology and Social Welfare 9.3 (1982):   388-390.

"The ERA is not enough for feminists, and it is too much for antifeminists.   The New Right has therefore been more singly committed to the defeat of the ERA than feminists have been singly committed to its ratification." (p. 389)

9-9.   Felsenthal, Carol.   The Sweetheart of the Silent Majority.   New York: Doubleday, 1981.

Phyllis Schlafly is the STOP-ERA Movement.   The "Phyllis Schlafly Report" was a perfect means for getting conservatives aroused.   She stopped the ERA and put together   an   unlikely   coalition   of   Catholics, Fundamentalists and Orthodox Jews. (p. 276)   Schlafly, a member of the Junior League, the Daughters of the American Revolution, a graduate of Radcliffe College, an anti-communist, an isolationist, with a passion for free enterprise and big defense budgets, took advantage of a genuine grass-roots movement on the political right to stop ratification of the ERA.

9-10.   Foss, Karen A.   "Origins of Contemporary Feminism: Source of Difficulty for the Equal Rights Amendment."   (1983) ED 222409.

Studying the development of three national feminist organizations, Foss finds that NOW's reliance on rational discussion caused it to emphasize the distribution of literature and the sponsoring of conferences.   These were not effective tools in organizing to win ratification of the ERA.

9-11.   Foss, Sonja K.   "Autopsy of the Equal Rights Amendment: Failure to Meet the Opposition's Rhetoric."   (1983)   ED 222410.

"The failure of the supporters of the Equal Rights Amendment to understand the rhetoric and world view of its opponents resulted in the defeat of the amendment." Anti-ERA   forces   argued   that   women   were   not discriminated against, that protective labor legislation protected women as did current alimony and child support laws.   Opponents   characterized proponents   as   radical militant 'libbers' who are aggressive and unrepresentative of American values.   ERA proponents violated the world view of its opponents and of male legislators, that women should remain in their proper sphere, the home, perform wifely duties, and ultimately be placed on a pedestal.

9-12. Frenier, Mariam Darce. "American Anti-Feminist Women." Women's Studies International Forum 7.6 (1984): 455-465.

> The author examines the rhetoric of American women who opposed the Ninteenth Amendment from 1890 to 1919 and the Equal Rights Amendment from 1970-1984. She finds that "Basic to the rhetoric of those opponents is a belief that men and women are so different from each other that they must be treated differently under the law." (p. 455) The rhetorical concerns of both groups are of the relationship between men and women, the family, and sexuality.

9-13. Ginsburg, Ruth Bader. "From No Rights, to Half Rights, to Confusing Rights." Human Rights 7 (1978): 12-14.

> In the last one hundred years, the Supreme Court has responded to gender-discrimination cases "uncertainly and unevenly." Its decisions "are a study in male hesitation and legal timidity." Not until 1971 when women brought numerous cases before the Court challenging sex discrimination in all legal areas, did the Court decide ad hoc, refusing to develop legal doctrine with which to deal with the all pervasive pattern of sex discrimination. The ERA would probably "relieve the Court's anxiety and end its hesitancy to shape new constitutional doctrine...."

9-14. Hacker, Andrew. "ERA-R.I.P." Harper's September 1980: 10-14.

> Hacker attributes the defeat of the ERA to it having become identified with women's liberation and its vague wording which was spelled out in the rallying cries of its supporters. Time and effort should be spent on consiousness-raising among young women before the ERA is reintroduced. "Women opposed the ERA because it jeopardized a way of life they had entered in good faith. And their legislators listened." (p. 14)

9-15. Howard, Holly Lynn. "Prejudice Against Women and Homosexuals." DAI 41 (1980): 1917B (University of Washington).

> Researching popular support for a range of civil rights legislation, Howard samples people's expectations and knowledge of proposed amendments. Her findings indicate that support or non-support for particular pieces of legislation often reflects prejudice against women and homosexuals.

9-16. Langer, Elinor. "Why Big Business is Trying to Defeat the ERA--the Economic Implications of Equality." Ms. May 1976: 64-66.

Opposition groups such as HOT DOG (Humanitarians Opposed to Degrading Our Girls) are funded by corporate interests for whom the equality of women would create an inelasticity in the labor force that profit margins could not bear. Among those corporate interests, the insurance industry stands out as a primary opponent.

9-17. McGlen, Nancy E. and Karen O'Connor. Women's Rights: The Struggle for Equality in the Nineteenth and Twentieth Centuries. New York: Praegar, 1983.

Women's groups did not counter the growing grass roots opposition to the ERA nor organize a strategy to advance ratification on the local or state levels. When the national ERA Ratification Council was finally formed, it was poorly funded and supported. ERAmerica was powerless to coordinate efforts among its organizations such as NOW, Business and Professional Women's Clubs, and the League of Women Voters. "The Anti-ERA movement did not have to be particularly large or well organized to achieve its aim.... The efforts of a relatively few persons with only one recognized leader helped to prevent the amendment's adoption." (p. 372-373) "It appears that the anti-ERA movement initially built primarily on two often inter-locking, pre-existing organizational structures: the religious right (fundamentalist, Mormon, and to a lesser extent, anti-abortion groups supported by the Roman Catholic Church) and the political right (most notably the John Birch Society, the American Party, and the Schlafly wing of the Republican Party.) These groups provided the state leadership in the anti-ERA movement." (p. 374) NOW has charged that the insurance industry which benefits from gender-based actuarial tables are major contributors to STOP-ERA. This funding was one of the key elements in contributing to the defeat of the ERA in Illinois. (p. 375)

9-18. Marlow, Carleton H. and Harrison M. Davis. The American Search for Women. Santa Barbara: Clio, 1976.

The authors oppose the ERA. They argue that its passage would interfere with a woman's nature and her highest function which is to fulfill her maternal instinct.

9-19. "The Rights Revolution." Editorial Research Reports.

Washington: Congressional Quarterly, 1978.

Chapter 3 describes the opposition's fear that the Amendment would overturn the traditional role of women and be detrimental to family, church, and nation. Opposition has been led by conservative political fundamentalist churches such as the Mormon Church and the hierarchy of the Catholic Church.   Phyllis Schlafly asserts "that American women have never had it so good. Why should we lower ourselves to 'equal rights' when we already have the status of special privilege."

9-20.   Schlafly, Phyllis.   The Power of the Positive Woman.   New York: Harcourt Brace, 1978.

"The positive woman looks upon her femaleness and her fertility as part of her purpose, her potential, and her power."   She finds that the fundamental error of the ERA is that it will mandate a genderfree, rigid, absolute equality of treatment between men and women.   It will not add any new rights to those already enacted.   The ERA will wipe out laws which protect and provide for women who are wives and mothers, and force them to leave their children and get jobs.   In the Phyllis Schlafly Report 6.4 (1974), (Box 618, Alton, IL 62002); she defends the rights of those women who do not want to compete on an equal basis with men.

9-21.   Solomon, Martha.   "The Positive Woman's Journey: A Mythical Analysis of the Rhetoric of STOP-ERA."   Quarterly Journal of Speech 65.3 (1979): 262-274.

"The success of STOP-ERA is testimony to the resilience of archetypal myths and to the skill by which Phyllis Schlafly, the acknowledged leader of STOP-ERA, has incorporated those myths into her rhetorical vision of the Positive Woman."   The romantic myths allow women to cope with "the sometimes disappointing and limited nature of human existence." (p. 271)

9-22.   Solomon, Martha.   "The Rhetoric of STOP-ERA: Fatalistic Reaffirmation."   The Southern Speech Communication Journal 44.1 (1978): 42-59.

STOP ERA women are described as women who accept reality and recognize privilege.   They are fatalistic and traditionally oriented.   Their rhetoric emphasizes the need to build security, affection, and belonging.

9-23.   Solomon,   Martha.   "Stopping   ERA: A   Pyrrhic   Victory."

Communication Quarterly 31.2 (1983): 109-117.

Schlafly's vision in the anti-ERA campaign was of "renewed allegiance to an eternal order mandated by Divine Providence and sustained by law and tradition." Assessing the STOP-ERA rhetoric, Solomon finds that it has won a pyrrhic victory having contributed to divisiveness and bitterness among women and between men and women and has encouraged narrow role expectations for men and women. "Despite its faith in the family and sterotypical roles, STOP-ERA argues widely for the necessity of laws to insure that men will support their wives and that wives in divorce cases will receive child support."

9-24.   White, Collis H.   Win or Lose? What You Should Know About the ERA.   Smithtown: Exposition, 1976.

White warns that should the ERA become law it would interfere with every aspect of life regardless of needs, qualifications and desires.   It would hurt relations between husband and wife, parent and child, family and church and business and professions.   It is the enemy of democracy.   It will give to Congress and to the federal courts unlimited power to use "due process" to regulate private and public affairs in matters of sex discrimination as it did in matters of race discrimination.   "The abolishment of the family will in effect be legalized by the ERA if it becomes law."

9-25.   Wohlenberg, Ernest H.   "Regional Attitudes Toward Passage of the Equal Rights Amendment." Texas Business Review January-February (1982): 6-10.

Regional differences showed that one third of all states failing to ratify the ERA are in the South Atlantic region. These states are traditionally slow to support innovative legislation. This area extending through the Sunbelt to Utah views the ERA as weakening the family. The states refusing to support the ERA also opposed the Nineteenth Amendment and the Twenty-Sixth Amendment. Wohlenberg dismisses people's claim that ERA opponents feared passage of ERA would threaten male jobs as the Sunbelt has a booming economy. The strongest support for ERA was in the Frostbelt where states have declining economies.

9-26.   "Abortion Clause Fight Kills ERA." National Catholic Reporter
        25 November 1983: 4.

9-27.   "Administration Split Over an ERA Appeal." New York Times 10
        January 1982: IV, 8.

9-28.   Amiel, B. "Let's Raise the Spectre of Unisex Washrooms--and
        All That Implies." Macleans 14 July 1980: 49.

9-29.   "Anti-ERA Evangelist Wins Again." (Phyllis Schlafly) Time 3 July
        1978: 20.

9-30.   "Backlash Phenomenon." Vital Speeches 15 August 1976: 669.

9-31.   Beck, M. "Last Hurrah for the ERA?" Newsweek 13 July 1981:
        24.

9-32.   Bokowski, D. "Amending the Constitution: The Case of the
        Equal Rights Amendment." DAI 45 (1984): 2635A (Ohio
        State University).

9-33.   Boles, J. K. "The Coalescence of Controversy." DAI 37
        (1976): 7935A (University of Texas).

9-34.   "Bribe Suspect Ties Cash Offer to Vote." (Wanda Brandstetter)
        New York Times 23 August 1980: 5.

9-35.   Broughton, P. "A Eulogy for the ERA." Other Side 13 August
        1982: 131.

9-36.   "Bush Tells GOP Women Reagan Won't Budge on ERA."
        Washington Post December 1983: A3.

9-37.   "Can Phyllis Schlafly Sleep Easy At Last?" Glamour August
        1982: 52.

9-38.   Cherry, S. "Women Plan Post-Chicago Strategy, Discuss ERA
        Tactics." American Libraries March 1980: 142-144.

9-39.   "Chronology of Events Before Rejection." New York Times 23
        June 1982: I, 9.

9-40.   Cohodas, N. "The Elusive Three States." Congressional
        Quarterly Weekly Report 28 June 1980: 1813-1815.

9-41.   "A Conservative Answer to ERA." Christian Science Monitor 26
        May 1982: 23.

9-42.   "A Conservative Answer to ERA." (Letter) Christian Science
        Monitor 4 June 1982: 22.

9-43.   "Constitutional Shell Game; Equal Rights Amendment." National
        Review 28 October 1977: 1218.

9-44. "Deadline Time for ERA." New Republic 17 December 1977: 6+.

9-45. "Death Knell?" (Two rulings hurt ERA) Time 4 January 1982: 63.

9-46. "Defeat." Washington Post 17 November 1983: B1.

9-47. "Dismissal of ERA Ruling is Urged by Justice Agency." Wall
       Street Journal 15 January 1982: 23.

9-48. "Double Trouble for the Fading ERA." Newsweek 4 January
       1982: 62.

9-49. "End   of ERA?" New Republic 30 April 1977: 14-15.

9-50. "End   of the ERA?" (Illinois vote) Newsweek 19 June 1978: 34.

9-51. "End   of the Line for ERA; D.C. Votes?" U.S. News and World
       Report 2 April 1979: 10.

9-52. English, D. "Communist Feminist Conspiracy." Mother Jones
       April 1982: 5.

9-53. English, D. "The Future of Feminism." Mother Jones November
       1982: 7-8.

9-54. "Equal Rights Amendment Falters in Two States." New York
       Times 15 February 1979: A22.

9-55. "Equal Rights Amendment: Illinois House Delays Vote."
       Christian Science Monitor 16 May 1980: 2.

9-56. "The   Equal Rights Amendment: The Case Against." Christian
       Science Monitor 6 May 1980: 14.

9-57. "Equal Rights and Unfair Meddling." (Editorial) New York Times
       30 December 1981: A24.

9-58. "Equal Rights Bill Fails by a Five-Vote Margin in the House in
       Illinois." New York Times 19 June 1980: A18.

9-59. "Equal Rights Measure Fails in Georgia by 2-1 Margin."
       Christian Science Monitor 22 January 1982: 2.

9-60. "Equal Rights Plan's Foe Declares Victory." (Phyllis Schlafly)
       New York Times 14 March 1979: C14.

9-61. "Equal Rights Proposal Opposed by Prospective Solicitor
       General." (Rex E. Lee) New York Times 27 May 1981:
       A12.

9-62. "Equal Rights Proposal is Set Back in Virginia." New York
       Times 2 February 1982: A9.

9-63. "Equal Rights Rejected Again." (Oklahoma) New York Times 20

January 1982: A21.

9-64. "Equal Rights Stalemate for Illinois." New York Times 8 June
1980: IV, 4.

9-65. "Equal Rights: Why the Amendment Appears Doomed." U.S.
News and World Report 28 March 1977: 53.

9-66. "ERA: Be Prepared." (Editorial from the Boston Globe) Christian
Science Monitor 8 June 1983: 24.

9-67. "ERA, But Not This Way." (Editorial) Washington Post 15
November 1983: A14.

9-68. "The ERA Challenge to Carter--and Other Americans."
Christian Science Monitor 14 December 1979: 24.

9-69. "ERA Countdown: Illinois." Time 12 June 1978: 20.

9-70. "The ERA Death Rattle." Newsweek 14 June 1982: 32-34.

9-71. "ERA Death Watch." (Editorial) Wall Street Journal 17 June
1982: 28.

9-72. "ERA Defeat: Illinois." Time 19 June 1978: 31.

9-73. "ERA Dies." Time 5 July 1982: 29.

9-74. "ERA Drive for Ratification; Outlook Dim." Christian Science
Monitor 11 December 1979: 4.

9-75. "ERA: Early Afterthoughts." National Review 27 October 1978:
1324-1326.

9-76. "The ERA Fixation." (Letter) Washington Post 16 January 1983:
B6.

9-77. "ERA Impasse." (Letter) Wall Street Journal 30 July 1981: 25.

9-78. "The ERA Loses Two More Rounds." (Oklahoma and Georgia)
Time 1 February 1982: 18.

9-79. "ERA Marches On to Another Lose." (Illinois) Time 26 May
1980: 23.

9-80. "ERA Oops." National Review 13 June 1980: 704-706.

9-81. "The ERA: Promises, Promises." Washington Post 17 July
1983: C7.

9-82. "ERA--R.I.P.?" Nation 3 July 1982: 3-4.

9-83. "ERA Runs into a Roadblock." (Illinois and North Carolina
answer no again) Time 26 February 1979: 19.

9-84.   "ERA   Runs Into Illinois Scandal." (Wanda Brandstetter) New York Times 18 May 1980: IV, E3.

9-85.   "ERA   Skirmish   Intensifies   in   Illinois."   Christian   Science Monitor 23 May 1980: 10.

9-86.   "ERA   Troubles."   Time 27 March 1978: 16.

9-87.   "The   ERA: Unlucky Seven." (Illinois) Newsweek 3 July 1978: 24.

9-88.   "The   ERA: What Went Wrong?" (Letter) Wall Street Journal 7 July 1982: 21.

9-89.   "ERA's Death and Fear of New Women."   New York Times 29 August 1982: IV, 19.

9-90.   "ERA's   Lessons."   (What   Others   Say: Omaha   World-Herald Editorial) Christian Science Monitor 19 August 1982: 24.

9-91.   "ERA's Persistent Adversary--Uncertain Over Effect."   (Florida) Christian Science Monitor 23 June 1982: 5.

9-92.   "ERA's Time is Gone." (S. J. Ervin, Jr.)   New York Times 1 August 1983: A17.

9-93.   Ewbank, H. L.   Free Speech Yearbook.   (1983) ED 226397.

9-94.   Farr, L.   "Anti-ERA Hustle."   Ms.   April 1976: 19.

9-95.   "Fear   Campaign." (Letter) Christian   Science   Monitor 13 July 1982: 22.

9-96.   "Feminism's Heritage: Suffragist Grandmas Had It Tougher Than Their ERA Grandaughters." Christian Science Monitor 23 September 1981: B13.

9-97.   "The   Fettered Human Rights Champion." (Letter) New York Times 23 July 1980: A20.

9-98.   Fishman, W.   "For the Love of Money...Who Killed the ERA?" Other Side August 1982: 14-16.

9-99.   "Florida Rebuffs Equal Rights Bid."   New York Times 22 June 1982: A8.

9-100   Flynn, S.   "My Side." (Elizabeth Dole) Working Woman May 1981: 156-158.

9-101.   "Foes of Equal Rights Plan."   New York Times 14 October 1979: I, 26.

9-102.   Frakee, S.   "Women vs. Women."   Newsweek 25 June 1977: 34-35.

9-103.   "Georgia House Rejects Rights Amendments."   New York Times
         21 January 1982: A9.

9-104.   "Georgia Senate Defeats Equal Rights Proposal."   New York
         Times 22 January 1980: A12.

9-105.   Gerhardt, L.   "Sulking to Oblivion."   (Editorial) School Library
         Journal November 1979: 9.

9-106.   "Good Show Phyllis."   (Defeat of ERA) National Review 6 August
         1982:   940.

9-107.   "The Grand Old Ploys."   (Editorial) New York Times 18 July
         1980: A25.

9-108.   Haig, S.   "Why Labor is Fighting the ERA."   Militant 7
         December 1979:   13

9-109.   Harrison, B. G.   "The Women Who is Fighting the Law that
         Most Women Want."   (Phyllis Schlafly) McCall's April 1982:
         84-85.

9-110.   "Idaho and Arizona Contest U.S. Equal Rights Proposal."   New
         York Times 10 May 1979: A16.

9-111.   "Idaho Opens its Challenge Over Rights Amendment."   New
         York Times 14 May 1981: A15.

9-112.   "Illinois Defeats Rights Amendment."   New York Times 23 June
         1982: A12.

9-113.   "Illinois ERA Vote: Reagan Cheers it."   Christian Science
         Monitor 23 June 1980: 6.

9-114.   "Illinois Lawmaker Says No to ERA."   New York Times 13 May
         1980: B16.

9-115.   "Illinois Says No to ERA."   New York Times 22 June 1980: IV,
         E4.

9-116.   "Illinois Senator Blocks Pro-ERA Rules Change."   Christian
         Science Monitor 16 February 1979: 2.

9-117.   "Is the Equal Rights Amendment Dead?"   U.S. News and
         World Report 1 December 1975: 39.

9-118.   "James J. Kilpatrick on the ERA."   (Letter) Washington Post 25
         October 1983: A18.

9-119.   Johnson, D.   "Proof of Abortion--ERA Link."   National Catholic
         Reporter 6 July 1984: 27.

9-120.   "Jubilant Schlafly Hails Defeat of ERA in House."   Los Angeles
         Times 16 November 1983: I, 4.

9-121.   Julliard,   J.   "Politics   of   the   Equal   Rights   Amendment."
         Sociology and Social Research 65.2 (1981): 242-243.

9-122.   Kassell,   P.   S.   "Right-Wing   Conspiracy?"   (Abortion   rights and
         ERA   ratification)   New   Directions   for   Women   6   August
         1978: 7.

9-123.   Kilpatrick,   J.   J.   "Equal   Rights   Amendment"   Nation's Business
         September 1982: 16.

9-124.   Kondracke,   M.   "End   of   an   ERA?"   New   Republic   30   April   1977:
         14-16.

9-125.   Langer,   E.   "Why   Big   Business   is   Trying   to   Defeat   the   ERA."
         Ms.   May 1976: 4-6+.

9-126.   "Last Hurrah for the ERA?"   Newsweek 13 July 1981: 24-26.

9-127.   Lelyveld,   J.   "Should   Women   Be   Nicer   Than   Men?"   (Phyllis
         Schlafly)   New   York   Times   17 April 1977: 25.

9-128.   "Life in an Unratified Country."   Witness 65.4 (1982): 3+.

9-129.   "Macho-Republicans."   (Letter)   New   York   Times   18   July   1980:
         A24.

9-130.   "Madison Avenue Equality."   National Review 25 June 1976: 666.

9-131.   "Maureen   Reagan's   Challenge."   (Editorial)   Christian   Science
         Monitor 22 June 1980: 24.

9-132.   Miller,   J.   "ERA in Trouble."   Progressive May 1977: 8.

9-133.   "Missouri   Vote   Deals   Setback   to   the   Equal   Rights   Proposal."
         New   York   Times   13 February 1982: A6.

9-134.   "North   Carolina   Senate   Bars   Vote   on   Equal   Rights   Plan."   New
         York   Times   5 June 1982: A8.

9-135.   Norton,   E.   H.   "Good-Bye   ERA...Hello   Equality."   Human
         Rights 12 (1984): 24-25.

9-136.   "Oklahoma   Stalls   Vote   on   Rights   Amendment."   New   York   Times
         14 February 1979: B4.

9-137.   Oliver,   J.   "Federal ERA Scoreboard."   Ms.   March 1976: 94.

9-138.   "On   ERA."   (Phyllis   Schlafly   letter)   Christian   Science   Monitor
         12 April 1979: 22.

9-139.   O'Reilly,   J.   "The   Mysterious   and   True   Story   of   the   ERA   in
         Oklahoma."   Ms.   July-August 1982: 82-88.

9-140.   O'Reilly,   J.   "Schlafly's   Last   Fling."   Ms.   September   1982:

42-43.

9-141.   "Phyllis Schlafly."   Christian Science Monitor 25 June 1982: 22.

9-142.   "Poetic Justice for the ERA." (Editorial) New York Times 27
         January 1982: A24.

9-143.   "Politics Aside, Women Have a Way to Go." New York Times 4
         July 1982: IV, E4.

9-144.   Prida, D. "What is the ERA and Why Are They Saying All
         Those Terrible Things About it?" Nuestro December
         1980: 18.

9-145.   "Pros and Cons on ERA Issue." (Phyllis Schlafly et al. letter)
         Wall Street Journal 30 May 1979: 24.

9-146.   Prospects for Equal Rights Amendment Dim as Drive Fails in
         Key States." New York Times 21 March 1979: A1.

9-147.   Reed, C. "Death of the ERA." World Press Review July 1981:
         48.

9-148.   "Requiem for the ERA." Progressive May 1982: 9-10.

9-149.   Riese, T. J. "Post-Mortem on the ERA."   America 24 July
         1982: 45.

9-150.   "Rights Amendment is Defeated, 27-21, in Oklahoma Senate."
         New York Times 14 January 1982: A8.

9-151.   A Rights Amendment Vote Rescinded in South Dakota." New
         York Times 1 March 1979: A16.

9-152.   "Rights Plan Dead in Virginia." New York Times 17 February
         1982: A11.

9-153.   "Rights Plan Foes Celebrate its Difficulties with a Gala." New
         York Times 23 March 1979: A18.

9-154.   "Romney Speaks Again in Trouble." New York Times 30
         December 1979: IV, E4.

9-155.   "Scandal May Doom the ERA." Newsweek 2 June 1980: 40.

9-156.   Schlafly, P. "Question of Ratification of Equal Rights
         Amendment--Con." Congressional Digest 56.6-7 (1977):
         189+.

9-157.   Schipper, H. "Some Girls." (Interview with Phyllis Schlafly)
         Rolling Stone 26 November 1981: 23.

9-158.   "Senate in Florida Rejects Equal Rights Proposal." New York
         Times 25 May 1979: A10.

9-159.   "Taking the ERA Literally." Washington Post 14 October 1983:
          A27.

9-160.   "That ERA March." National Review 4 August 1978: 939.

9-161.   "Time Runs Out for Proposed Rights Amendment." New York
          Times 1 July 1982: A11.

9-162.   "Time's Up: ERA Ratification Deadline." National Review 25
          November 1977: 1344+.

9-163.   "A Troubled Decade for the ERA." Christian Science Monitor
          22 March 1982: 5.

9-164.   "Twilight of the ERA Era." Time 13 July 1981: 17.

9-165.   "Two   Black   Legislators   in   Illinois   May   Not   Aid   Rights
          Amendment." New York Times 8 June 1980: A30.

9-166.   "The Unmaking of an Amendment." Time 25 April 1977: 89-90.

9-167.   "U.S. Opposes NOW on Quick Equal Rights Appeal." New York
          Times 6 January 1982: A9.

9-168.   Van   Gelder,   L.   "400,000   Vote   Misunderstanding."   Ms.
          March 1976: 67.

9-169.   "Victory is Bittersweet for Architect of Amendment's Downfall."
          (Phyllis Schlafly) New York Times 1 July 1982: A11.

9-170.   "Vote by Illinois Senate Backs Defeat of Equal Rights Move."
          New York Times 27 June 1982: A22.

9-171.   "Vote Kills Rights Amendment." New York Times 14 February
          1980: A22.

9-172.   "Vote Set in Illinois House on Rights Proposal Today." New
          York Times 14 May 1980: A16.

9-173.   Wall, J. M. "The Gospel According to Schlafly." (Editorial)
          Christian Century 11 April 1979: 396-397.

9-174.   "What Do Women Want."   National Review 8 August 1980:
          943-945.

9-175.   "Why ERA Could Hinge on Vote in Illinois." Christian Science
          Monitor 23 April 1980: 3.

9-176.   "Why ERA Failed." Christian Science Monitor 30 June 1982: 10.

9-177.   "Why the ERA Frightens Women." Mademoiselle February 1976:
          18+; March 1976: 54+.

9-178.   "Why the Equal Rights Amenment is Stalled."   Wall Street

Journal 20 July 1981: 16.

9-179. "Will ERA Loss Hurt GOP?" Christian Science Monitor 11 July 1980: 10.

9-180. Will, G. F. "Stacking the Deck on ERA." Newsweek 14 November 1977: 128.

9-181. Will, L. "Equal Rights at the Schlaflys' Means that Phyllis Shines in Public and Fred Reigns at Home." People 30 March 1981: 103-106.

9-182. Williams, R. M. "Women Against Women." Saturday Review 25 June 1977: 6-13.

9-183. "With or Without ERA." (Editorial) Christian Science Monitor 28 December 1981: 24.

9-184. Wohl, L. "ERA: What the Hell Happened in New York?" Ms. March 1976: 64.

9-185. Wohl, L. "ERA: What If it Fails?" Ms. November 1979: 64-65.

9-186. Wolfe, H. B. "Backlash Phenomenon." (Address) Vital Speeches 15 August 1976: 669-672.

9-187. Wolff, C. G. "A Woman's Place." Saturday Review 25 June 1977: 8-10.

9-188. "Woman Convicted of Vote Bribe is Ordered to Do Public Service." (Wanda Brandstetter) New York Times 8 November 1980: A6.

9-189. "Women and Leadership: Phyllis Schlafly." New York Times 24 January 1980: C2.

9-190. "Women Vote Against ERA." National Catholic Reporter 29 December 1978: 3.

9-191. "Women's Organization Assails 101 as Equal Rights Defectors." (NOW) New York Times 27 June 1982: A18.

10 Television News Coverage

10-1. Tuesday, August 10, 1976, ABC, 5:00 P.M.

> Ron Miller reports from the floor of the Republican Party Convention in Kansas City, Missouri, saying that the Reagan forces oppose Ford's support for the ERA plank in the party platform. Phyllis Schlafly says that if the stand against ERA is adopted it will neutralize resentment over President and Ms. Ford's intimate involvement with the radical women's movement: and that Ms. Ford's statement on behalf of ERA indicate a tolerance for fornication and illegal pot smoking. A supporter of ERA says that support for the ERA will welcome women into the Republican Party and put women in the Constitution.

10-2. Wednesday, August 11, 1976, CBS, 5:30 P.M.

> From Kansas City, Bill Plant says that Ford backers expected the Subcommittee on Human Rights and Responsibilities to endorse the ERA plank but, instead, it voted to take no stand on ERA. It recommended enforcement of anti-sex discrimination laws. The compromise on the platform planks was necessary because of the close contest between Ford and Reagan on Ford's nomination.

10-3. Thursday, August 13, 1976, ABC, 5:30 P.M.

> At the Republican Party Convention, Representative Millicent Fenwick (R. NJ) speaks in the platform subcommittee on human rights meeting in Kansas City. She says that in the bicentennial year we should not be debating women's equality. Frances Weidman, a Reagan delegate, says that women have preferential treatment which ERA would destroy. Anti-ERA demonstrators are shown carrying signs which read, "Children need love not day care," "Abort ERA."

10-4. Wednesday, December 8, 1976, ABC, 5:00 P.M.

> Following the Supreme Court's ruling denying pregnancy as a disability, Representative Ed Koch (D. NY) calls for ratification of the ERA. The Equal Rights Amendment "will end all discrimination against women based on sex." Film footage shows women at work.

10-5.   Wednesday, December 15, 1976, NBC, 5:30 P.M.

> Referring to the recent Supreme Court ruling on pregnancy disability, Senator Birch Bayh (D. IN) says that Congress has said consistently that women should be treated equally.   He calls for ratification of the Equal Rights Amendment.

10-6.   Tuesday, January 18, 1977, ABC, 5:00 P.M.

> Barbara Walters announces the approval of the ERA in the Indiana state senate making Indiana the thirty-fifth state to pass the ERA.   The background graphic says "Important Victory for ERA: breaking of log jam."

10-7.   Tuesday, January 18, 1977, CBS, 5:30 P.M.

> Covering the Indiana passage of the ERA, Renee Poussaint says that Indiana women have worked against the re-election of anti-ERA legislators.   In the Indiana Senate, there is a slim democratic majority and the ERA passed by a vote of 26-24.

10-8.   Friday, February 4, 1977, ABC, 5:00 P.M.

> In a twenty-second news item, Harry Reasoner reports on several hundred demonstrators against ERA outside the White House where Phyllis Schlafly says that President Carter is using the power of his office in favor of the Amendment.   In Savannah, Georgia, other opponents of ERA announce that they will boycott Girl Scout cookies because the Girl Scouts have endorsed the ERA.

10-9.   Tuesday, February 8, 1977, CBS, 5:30 P.M.

> Terry Drinkwater describes the status of the ERA in Nevada against film footage of showgirls, card dealers and a statue of the most powerful madame in Virginia City.   He says that President Carter has sent telegrams in favor of ratification, and the Mormon Church against. Nevada State Senator Margie Foote says the Amendment isn't necessary, "Women can do anything they choose to do."   State Senator William Raggio says that the "Amendment is not sinister, as some say, but it's important to a sizeable segment of American women." Drinkwater comments on the national vote on ERA hinges on Nevada, and notes the irony of this happening in a state where the image of women is as sex symbols.

10-10. Wednesday, February 9, 1977, NBC, 5:30 P.M.

The graphic used in the background of David Brinkley's news report on ERA shows the female biological symbol equal to the male biological symbol.

10-11. Tuesday, March 1, 1977, NBC, 5:30 P.M.

Reporting on the defeat of the ERA in the North Carolina senate, David Brinkley says that the "NBC polls show a small majority, 57 percent, support ERA, (63 percent of men and 51 percent of women)." The NBC graphic shows the biological sign for women equaling that for men and captioned "Another Defeat."

10-12. Wednesday, March 16, 1977, ABC, 5:00 P.M.

Barbara Walters claims that the defeat of the ERA in the Missouri state legislature is a major setback.   ERA supporters do not think they can get the necessary support needed this year for ratification.

10-13. Tuesday, March 22, 1977, ABC, 5:00 P.M.

Barbara Walters announces a setback for ERA in South Carolina. Phyllis Schlafly speaks about "massive federal spending and White House interference" in support of ERA. Pro-ERA forces hold a news conference and blame Schlafly for delaying passage of the ERA. Viewers are reminded that the outlook is not good.

10-14. Friday, March 25, 1977, ABC, 5:00 P.M.

Harry Reasoner says that Attorney General Griffin Bell finds that once a state ratifies the ERA, it can not withdraw ratification.

10-15. Wednesday, April 13, 1977, CBS, 5:30 P.M.

The legislature turns down the ERA in Florida. It loses by two votes. Issues raised in the debate include homosexual marriages, unisex toilets, and women in combat.   State Senator Lori Wilson condemns ERA's opponents in the South as the good-ole-boys who are afraid for their manhood. Betty Friedan asks why the senators have betrayed their consitutents who support ERA. Walter Cronkite says that chances for ERA passage are narrow.

10-16.   Sunday, April 24, 1977, CBS, 5:00 P.M.

Eleanor Smeal, newly elected president of the National Organization of Women (NOW), is introduced as a Pittsburgh housewife and mother of two who pledges a multiplicity of strategies for ERA ratification. She is shown beside her engineer husband and says that she does not mind having a full-time employed spouse.

10-17.   Friday, July 18, 1980, ABC, 5:30 P.M.

President Carter announces support for the ERA in the Rose Garden before the American Legion's women's group.

10-18.   Friday, August 26, 1977, ABC, 5:30 P.M.

The lead story shows the women's rights march from the National Archives to the White House. President Carter meets with the women and pledges to seek ratification in the three remaining states. Reporter Charles Gibson says this is a movement of women who have not marched before and have not been involved in other issues.

10-19.   Thursday, September 1, 1977, CBS, 5:30 P.M.

Appearing before Senator Proxmire's committee, women in the armed forces say that the issue of women in combat translates into an economic issue where women are denied advancement and promotional opportunities. The women mention retired General Westmoreland's comment that women are not fit to fight along with men and General Hershey's remark that women are defective men. This hearing is held on the eve of graduation of ten women from the Air Force Academy who will not be allowed to fly combat missions.

10-20.   Wednesday, October 26, 1977, CBS, 5:30 P.M.

The impact of the pro-ERA boycott on major convention cities such as Miami, Atlanta, New Orleans, and Las Vegas is severe. Chicago reports losses of fifteen million dollars. Eleanor Smeal, president of NOW, reports the growing support of labor and civil rights groups for the boycott.

10-21.   Tuesday, November 1, 1977, NBC, 5:30 P.M.

A spokesperson for Attorney General Griffin Bell says that Congress has the right to extend the deadline for ratification of the Equal Rights Amendment. Both Smeal and Schlafly are interviewed. John Chancellor says that 55 percent of the nation supports passage of the ERA. But men continue to lead women in support of ERA. He says the extension of ERA promises to be as divisive as the ERA.

10-22.   Thursday, November 17, 1977, NBC, 5:30 P.M.

Describing the International Women's Year Conference in Houston, Carole Simpson interviews Barbara Smith who leads the Mormon's Women's Auxiliary Relief Society. Ms. Smith says that women's liberation would lead to the downfall of American society and would encourage homosexuals to expect preferential treatment.

10-23.   Friday, November 18, 1977, ABC, 5:30 P.M.

Pro-ERA marathon runners (including Bella Abzug) are shown running for the ERA at the start of the Houston Conference. Bettina Gregory reports on the opposition at the Conference. Feminists are accused of rigging votes to prevent election of anti-ERA delegates. Calling themselves pro-family, the opposition groups take out ads in the local newspapers. One ad "Mommy, when I grow up, can I be a lesbian?" is shown. Eighty percent of the delegates support the National Plan of Action presented at Houston.

10-24.   Friday, November 18, 1977, NBC, 5:30 P.M.

David Brinkley speaks about the International Woman's Year Conference in Houston. He says there is a long list of issues, questions and disagreements to be discussed, such as abortion, homosexuality, and the ERA.

10-25.   Sunday, November 20, 1977, NBC, 5:30 P.M.

While NBC shows film of enthusiastic multi-racial supporters of ERA snake-dancing after ERA approval was voted, Reporter George Lewis asks how seriously all those male legislators in Washington will take the recommendations of all these women in Houston. Opponents say that the Conference has strengthened their resolve to defeat the ERA. ERA is tied to many issues, here, race equality, gay rights, and abortion rights.

10-26.   Thursday, December 8, 1977, CBS, 5:30 P.M.

        Roger Mudd speaks of the support for the ERA at the Houston Conference but of dwindling support nationwide. There is division among women about asking for a seven year extension. Representative Elizabeth Holtzman (D. NY) says that seven years is as arbitrary as fourteen years: why not wait another seven years to seek ratification and to continue the national debate? She says that states are stalling and there is a lot of misinformation on the ERA.

10-27.   Tuesday, January 3, 1978, CBS, 5:30 P.M.

        Having studied the matter of women in combat support units, a Pentagon spokesperson says that women can be used effectively but thinks that the decision on women is a political decision and will have to be made by the public, the politicans and the army's senior management.

10-28.   Tuesday, February 14, 1978, CBS, 5:30 P.M.

        In an ERA update, Bill Plant surveys its defeat in South Carolina, Alabama, Georgia, and Virginia. ERA supporters hope for passage in Florida and Illinois. Idaho, Nebraska, and Tennessee voted to rescind. Sheila Greenwald of ERAmerica outlines plans to press Congress for action to extend the deadline.

10-29.   Monday, March 20, 1978, CBS, 5:30 P.M.

        The Kentucky state legislature rescinds ERA approval. The action was overturned by the Lieutenant Governor Thelma Stovall in the absence of the governor.

10-30.   Thursday, June 22, 1978, NBC, 5:30 P.M.

        NOW president Eleanor Smeal argues for deadline extension to continue the national debate. STOP-ERA co-chairperson Kathy Teague states the position against deadline extension. Thomas Railsback (R. IL) argues that rescinding approval be allowed in return for extending the deadline. Representative Don Edwards (D. CA) says rescinding is unconstitutional. The vote to extend the deadline is before the House Judiciary Committee.

10-31.   Sunday, July 9, 1978, NBC, 5:30 P.M.

This news segment begins with the intertwined biological signs for men and women and an anti-ERA demonstration. Bella Abzug calls on Congress to share women's anger and anguish, to stop delaying tactics, and to vote for extension. She calls on President Carter to make a national speech in support of ERA.

10-32.   Sunday, July 15, 1979, NBC, 5:30 P.M.

Covering the National Women's Political Caucus Convention in Cincinnati, Ohio, where Lynda Johnson Robb (chair of the President's Advisory Commission on Women) and Patricia Harris (Secretary of Housing and Urban Development) endorse the ERA: Art Kent says that the ratification of the ERA is the major goal of organized women's groups.

10-33.   Tuesday, July 18, 1978, ABC, 5:30, P.M.

The ERA deadline extension is before the House Judiciary Committee. Committee chair Peter Rodino (D. NJ) compares the pressure placed on the Committee to Watergate times. Representative Barbara Jordon (D. TX) says the Committee has the power and the authority to extend the deadline. Representative Elizabeth Holtzman (D. NY) says that we are denying women their human rights before an international forum.

10-34.   Tuesday, July 18, 1978, CBS, 5:30 P.M.

The House Judiciary Committee in a compromise vote extends the ratification deadline by three years and three months. Representative Barbara Jordan (D. TX) says she has no problem with a seven year extension or a generation of time to allow women to join the community of human kind.

10-35.   Thursday, August 3, 1978, NBC, 5:30 P.M.

Former Senator Sam Ervin (D. NC), a constitutional expert, says one thing the Constitution does not allow is extending the deadline for ratification of the ERA.

10-36.   Wednesday, October 4, 1978, ABC, 5:00 P.M.

Pro-ERA forces win a major victory as the Senate votes against allowing states to rescind their ratification of ERA. An anti-ERA lobbyist from Tennessee says that she has come to lobby for her home, family, god, and country: "Our country will fall." A Pro-ERA lobbyist from Pennsylvania says it is heartbreaking that she has to fight for the same constitutional protections every male citizen is born with.

10-37.   Friday, October 6, 1978, CBS, 5:30 P.M.

STOP-ERA leader, Phyllis Schlafly, says that the proposal to extend the ERA approval deadline is a tactic of desperation by ERA supporters who know that they are losing at the state level. After the Senate vote to extend the deadline, Representative Elizabeth Holtzman (D. NY) says that ERA supporters were told they could not do it but they beat the opposition every step of the way.

10-38.   Friday, October 20, 1978, CBS, 5:30 P.M.

President Carter is shown signing the resolution extending the ratification deadline. He says he wishes to demonstrate again, as strongly as he can, his full support for ratification.

10-39.   Saturday, November 17, 1979, CBS, 5:30 P.M.

Sonia Johnson, a member of the Mormon Church, is accused of heresy by the Church because of her campaign for ERA which is said to undermine Church doctrine. Emerging from her five-hour Church hearing, Johnson says that when the Bishop takes as strong a political stand as he has, and he believes he has been inspired by God; she disagrees.

10-40.   Wednesday, December 5, 1979, NBC, 5:30 P.M.

Reading from her letter of excommunication, Sonia Johnson says the Church condemns her because of her activity of behalf of ERA. Church spokesperson L. Don LeFevre says that the Church is not against her support of ERA but her support included attacks against the Church. He says that there are Mormon church members in good standing who support the ERA.

10-41.   Thursday, December 13, 1979, CBS, 5:30 P.M.

On the eve of his re-election bid, President Carter says that the ERA is the single most important human rights issue in the country. NOW's executive board votes not to support Carter for re-election, although other women's groups do.   Carter aides say that NOW is pro-Kennedy.

10-42.   Friday, January 5, 1979, CBS, 5:30 P.M.

The AFL-CIO announces it will move its annual convention from Florida to Washington D.C. in support of NOW's ERA boycott of non-ratifying states.

10-43.   Tuesday, February 27, 1979, CBS, 5:30 P.M.

The South Dakota state legislature votes to rescind its ratification of the ERA.

10-44.   Wednesday, February 6, 1980, ABC, 5:00 P.M.

Reporter Bettina Gregory asks whether President Carter will register females as long as he is bringing back draft registration for males.   Admiral Elmo Zumwalt who supports ERA announces Carter's plans to ask Congress for authority to draft women. Zumwalt supports the registration of women.

10-45.   Monday, February 18, 1980, NBC, 5:30 P.M.

As the presidential election campaign of 1980 starts, John Chancellor says ERA will be an issue.   Governor Jerry Brown (D. CA), Senator Edward Kennedy (D. MA), and President Carter endorse ERA.   Only presidential candidate Ronald Reagan opposes ERA.

10-46.   Friday, March 28, 1980, NBC, 5:30 P.M.

Claiming losses of nineteen million dollars in convention and tourist revenue, Missouri files suit to contest NOW's economic boycott.   The federal appeals court in St. Louis finds that NOW's action is protected by the First Amendment.

10-47.   Saturday, May 10, 1980, NBC, 6:30 P.M.

The ratification drive for ERA moves to Illinois.   An ERA rally in Chicago is addressed by Mayor Jane Byrne, Eleanor Smeal (NOW), Jesse Jackson (Operation PUSH) and Gloria Steinem (Ms.)   Reporter Norma Quarles says that tens of thousands marched to show their support for ERA.   Illinois is the only northern industrial state not to have ratified the ERA.   Phyllis Schlafly (STOP-ERA) speaks to another rally in Springfield, IL, and says "that little pressure groups are not going to deny us our right to make reasonable common sense differences in treatment between men and women.   They are not going to take our daughters and send them out to fight this country's wars."

10-48.   Wednesday, June 18, 1980, NBC, 5:30 P.M.

Phyllis   Schlafly   (STOP-ERA)   accuses   Carter   of outside interference and of using public funds to force legislators to vote yes when they want to vote no.

10-49.   Tuesday, July 8, 1980, ABC, 5:30 P.M.

Meeting in Detroit for their presidential nominating convention, the Republican Party debates endorsing the ERA.   Candidate Ronald Reagan says that although he opposes ERA, he will allow it to stand in the party platform because of the Party's historical commitment to it.

10-50.   Wednesday, July 9, 1980, ABC, 5:30 P.M.

Betty Heitman replaces Mary Crisp as Republican National Committttee co-chairperson.   Crisp says she was drummed out of the the Party which she charged with burying the rights of women.   Congresswoman Margaret Heckler (R. MA) says not supporting the ERA could cost the Party the election.

10-51.   Tuesday, October 14, 1980, ABC, 5:30, P.M.

While speaking in Idaho Falls in an attempt to mollify pro-ERA voters, presidential candidate, Ronald Reagan promises to appoint a woman to the Supreme Court.

10-52.   Tuesday, June 30, 1980, ABC, 5:30 P.M.

Film   footage   shows   pro-ERA   rallies   around   the country.   Speakers include Alan Alda, Eleanor Smeal, Valerie Harper, and Marlo Thomas.

10-53.   Monday, October 12, 1981, ABC. 5:30 P.M.

A pro-ERA rally is held in front of the Lincoln Memorial.   Former first ladies Betty Ford and Lady Bird

Johnson speak.   Johnson compares the drive to ratify the
ERA to the civil rights struggle.

10-54.   Tuesday, June 8, 1982, NBC, 5:30 P.M.

As Illinois prepares to vote of the ERA, seven women
fast for twenty-two days.   They are shown in wheel
chairs beneath their banner, "Women hunger for justice."
Phyllis Schlafly says that ERA will not pass in this
century.   ERA supporters march and chant, "Thompson
[Governor of Illinois] remember, we vote in November."

10-55.   Wednesday, June 30, 1982, 5:30 P.M.

Reporter Ken Bode reviews the ratification effort.
Moral Majority leader Jerry Falwell says girls would end
up in combat.   Phyllis Schlafly says ERA is a direct
attack on the family structure.   Bode recalls the National
Women's Conference in Houston, and says that linking
ERA to more radical demands was damaging.

10-56.   Tuesday, November 15, 1983, CBS, 5:30 P.M.

Dan Rather reports that the attempt to restart the
ERA in the House of Representatives failed.   Kathy
Wilson of the National Women's Political Caucus says that
Republicans have been influenced by President Reagan's
right-wing tone.

ARTICLES ON MEDIA COVERAGE

10-57. Butler, Matilda and William Paisley. "Equal Rights Coverage in Magazines." Journalism Quarterly 55.1 (1978): 157-160.

The authors analyzed the coverage of ERA in twenty-eight magazines during the summer of 1976. Most of the articles (73 percent) favored ERA. Fourteen percent were neutral, eleven percent presented both pro and con arguments and three percent were against the ERA. The issues most often focused on were employment, divorce, marriage, and the draft.

10-58. Farley, Jennie. "Women's Magazines and the ERA: Friend or Foe." Journal of Communications 28.1 (1978): 187-193.

Farley reports on the results of an effort of six women's magazines' editors to encourage other women's magazines to publish an article on the ERA in their July 1976 issues. Thirty-nine magazines responded. She analyzes the results on the basis of the amount of coverage, type of magazine, editorial policy, circulation, and the social class of readership.

10-59. Hill, D.B. "Letter Opinion on ERA." Public Opinion Quarterly 45.3 (1981): 384-392.

This paper compares opinions expressed in published letters to the editor with public opinion on ERA. After taking a national sample of 92 daily newspapers, the author found no substantial difference between letter opinion and public opinion, and little support for the hypothesis that newspaper policies bias letter opinion. (Modified abstract)

10-60. Jarrard, Mary W. "Emerging ERA Patterns in Editorials on Southern Daily Newspapers." Journalism Quarterly 57.4 (1980): 606-611.

Surveying southern editorials on women's rights issues and the ERA, Jarrard found conservative rhetoric used to present women's issues and the Equal Rights Amendment.

10-61.   "All   for   ERA."   (Support   from   women's   magazines)   *Time*   29
          October 1979:   99.

10-62.   "Caroline   McKettrick   Study   Finds   Media   [newspapers]   Didn't
          Tell How Elected Women Stood on ERA."   *Media Report to*
          Women May 1983: 12-13.

10-63.   "Debora Becker Study Finds *Washington Post* and *New York*
          Times Still Don't Give Elemental Facts on ERA."   *Media*
          Report to Women January 1984: 9-10.

10-64.   "Lisa Sarasohn Study Finds *New York Times* Did Not Tell Basic
          Facts About ERA."   *Media Report to Women* September
          1982: 1+.

10-65.   " *Los Angeles Times* News Stories Did Not Give Basic Factual
          Information on ERA."   *Media Report to Women* September
          1978: 1+.

10-66.   "Sally Sacher Study: *Washington Post* Gave No Basic Data for
          ERA Decision-Making."   *Media Report to Women* March
          1981: 9.

10-67.   "Sandra Hagerty Asks Whether *Chicago Tribune* Readers Were
          Given Basic ERA Facts."   *Media Report to Women* July
          1982: 1+.

10-68.   Smith,   L.   L.   "Coverage   or   Cover-Up: A   Comparison   of
          Newspaper Coverage of the 19th Amendment and the
          Equal Rights Amendment." ED 246422 (1984).

10-69.   Smith,   L.   L.   "NOW vs.   STOP-ERA: Unequal Messages on the
          Equal Rights Amendment." ED 246434 (1984).

11   After 1982

11-1.   Goldstein, Leslie Friedman.   "The ERA and American Public Policy."   (Paper presented at the annual meeting of the American Political Science Association.) September, 1984.

Goldstein calls for congressional action on the Equal Rights Amendment.   She says this is not a matter for the Supreme Court, as the Court should not articulate public policy.

11-2.   Langer, Howard J.   "The Women's Movement: What NOW?"   Social Education Education 47.2 (1983): 112-121.

This is an interview with Eleanor Smeal, the President of the National Organization for Women (NOW) from 1977 to 1982.   The topics discussed include: ERA, gender gap, sexual harrassment, and Phyllis Schlafly.

11-3.   Oliphant, Lincoln C.   "Toward a New ERA?"   National Review 24 June 1983: 742-745.

The 1972 Equal Rights Amendment failed because its wording was both too vague in some areas and too specific in others.   Oliphant suggests that if a new ERA is introduced, it should be worded differently.   The new version should call for scrutiny of sex-based classifications but not prohibit them, because a "heterosexual society requires some classifications by sex."   Failure to reintroduce the ERA implies a willingness to risk having the Supreme Court make the decisions on sex discrimination.

11-4.   O'Reilly, Jane.   "After the ERA: What Next."   Perspectives Fall, 1982:   16-19.

The failure of the ERA despite ratification in 35 states (or 72 percent of the nation's population), shows a "lingering distrust of the idea of equal women."   The ERA failed because the majority which supported it was not evenly distributed geographically and was not "politically insistent."   The failure of the ERA reflects a "mean-spirited disinclination to progress which should be sobering to all concerned with civil rights."   The author sees promise in the large number of women graduating from law school who expect equal treatment.   She urges the defense of progress against the profit and habit of sex discrimination. (p. 19)

11-5. Rhode, Deborah L. "It May Have Been Fruitless, But...." Student Lawyer 12 (1984): 12-15.

> "In the final analysis, the ERA was a dispute less over constitutional entitlements than cultural dominance." It reflected society's deep-seated ambivalence about the role of women in America. Opponents saw ERA as not simply an assault on sexual discrimination but on all sexual distinctions. "Equality, as opponents perceive it, constituted a denial of roles that were biologically determined and culturally appropriate." (p. 12) Proponents failed to make a clear case for attacking gender-domination not gender-difference. They learned too late to stick to boycotts and ballots rather than public relations.

11-6. Rivers, Caryl. "Justice for All: The Second Equal Rights Amendment." Wilson Library Bulletin December 1982: 288-292.

> The most powerful roadblock to ERA ratification was the fear of change. In order for a new effort at the ERA to be successful, this fear must be overcome. The image of the ERA as a family destroyer and changer of women to a non-nurturing role must be changed.

11-7. Steinem, Gloria et al. "Losing a Battle But Winning the War?" Ms. January 1983: 35-39.

> Steinem analyzes the radicalization of women after the defeat of the ERA. This defeat was not a resounding victory for the conservative right wing. The moral majority and the anti-abortion political action committees proved lethal in targeted areas but only turned out three percent of the 1980 vote, a record low voting year. The effect of women's groups on the 1980 elections was somewhat harder to judge. However the total turnout did increase more than three percent from 1978. Several candidates who were preferred by women and supported women's issues did win including Mario Cuomo as Governor of New York and Roberta Fox (D. FL). Steinem sees a positive trend but women still have to register and learn how to deliver the vote.

11-8. Tribe, Laurence H. "Testimony Before the Subcommittee on Civil and Constitutional Rights." (House Committee on the Judiciary, regarding H.J. Res. 1: The Equal Rights Amendment.) Harvard Civil Rights-Civil Liberties Law Review 19.1 (1984): 15-20.

This article presents the testimony previously submitted in 1983 to the House Judiciary Committee. Tribe says that it is just as hard to predict what would happen to the Constitution with the ERA as without it. Among the arguments against ERA which he finds irrelevant is denial of tax benefits to single sex schools. (Congress has broad discretionary tax powers already.) The only criticism of ERA which should be taken seriously is that gender-equality should not be a controlling legal principle.

11-9.   Tucker, Marna S.   "A 'National Disgrace': This Time, the ERA will Pass."   Human Rights 11 (1983): 13+.

The reintroduction of the ERA finds a much less friendly forum before the Senate Subcommittee on the Constitution, chaired by Orrin Hatch (R. UT). Nonetheless, Tucker, Chair of the American Bar Association's section on Individual Rights and Responsibilities; says that ERA will pass next time because sex discrimination continues and is widespread.

11-10.   U.S.   Commission on Civil Rights.   State of Civil Rights, 1957-1983.   (The Final Report of the U.S. Commission on Civil Rights).   November 1983.

Once again the Commission goes on record supporting the ERA and cites beneficial changes for women. Despite the failure of the ERA to win ratification in 1982, "the Commission believes that its resurrection and incorporation into the Constitution are worthy goals of possible achievement." (p. 80)

11-11. "After ERA: A Search for New Direction Begins." Christian Science Monitor 25 June 1982: 1.

11-12. "After the ERA: Rival Groups Ponder Divergent Women's Rights Strategies." Wall Street Journal 25 June 1982: 1.

11-13. Askin, S. "Abortion Clause Fight Kills ERA." National Catholic Reporter 25 November 1983: 4.

11-14. Avery, P. A. "With ERA Dying, What's Ahead for Women's Groups." US News and World Report 28 June 1982: 55.

11-15. "Ballot Issues; Abortion and ERA." Ms. December 1984: 76.

11-16. Bresler, R. J. "Feminist Politics After ERA." USA Today September 1982: 8-10.

11-17. Cassell, K. "ALA and the ERA: Looking Back on the Association's Political and Fiscal Involvement." American Libraries December 1982: 690-695.

11-18. Cohodas, N. "ERA Dies as Deadline Passes: Amendment Is Reintroduced." Congressional Weekly Report 3 July 1982: 1585-1586.

11-19. "Constitution Isn't Place for Remediation of Bias." Wall Street Journal 25 January 1984: 32.

11-20. "Despite Defeat, Equal Rights Measure Again Is Offered in Congress." New York Times 15 July 1982: 16.

11-21. Drinan, R. F. National Catholic Reporter 18 June 1982: 2.

11-22. Ehrenreich, B. "Defeating the ERA: A Right-Wing Mobilization of Women." Journal of Sociology and Social Welfare 9.3 (1982): 391-398.

11-23. Eisler, R. "Women's Rights and Human Rights." Humanist 41 November-December 1980: 4-11.

11-24. "Eleanor Smeal Talks About Women and Politics." (Homemakers' rights) Christian Science Monitor 20 March 1984: 27.

11-25. English, D. "The Future of Feminism." Mother Jones November 1982: 7-9.

11-26. "Equal Rights Supporters Plan to Re-Offer Measure." New York Times 23 March 1982: 12.

11-27. "ERA--A Fresh Start." US News and World Report 27 June 1983: 66.

11-28. "ERA, Abortion Linked." National Catholic Reporter 14 September 1984: 8.

11-29.   "ERA Again." Washington Post 5 January 1983: B1.

11-30.   "ERA Is Back--Warts and All." Washington Post 26 January
         1983: A21.

11-31.   "E.R.A. is Dead, But the 10 Year Fight for It Brought Women
         a Long, Long Way." People 5 July 1982: 32-37.

11-32.   "ERA Round 2: Now the Issues Are Economic." Business Week
         1 August 1983: 92-94.

11-33.   "ERA Setback in the House." (Letter) Los Angeles Times 25
         November 1983: II, 6.

11-34.   "ERA Strategy: Is There Life After Tsongas?" (Senator Paul
         Tsongas) National Review 8 July 1983: 794-796.

11-35.   "ERA Tacticians Need Dolly's Spouse." (Letter) Wall Street
         Journal 27 December 1983: 13.

11-36.   "ERA II: A Chance to Do It Right." Washington Post 11 June
         1983: A23.

11-37.   "ERA Under Tight Rule, Fails in the House." American Bar
         Association Journal January 1984: 46.

11-38.   "For Most Americans, Passage of the ERA Is Just a Matter of
         Time." Business Week 1 August 1983: 92-94.

11-39.   Holleman, E. "The ERA: How Did We Let It Go Down the
         Drain." Other Side August 1982: 10-12.

11-40.   Hoodbhoy, N. "A Revivied ERA." Guardian 36.5 (1983): 5.

11-41.   "House Applause for ERA II Stops in the Middle of the Aisle."
         Washington Post 4 January 1983: A3.

11-42.   "House ERA Defeat Gives Democrats Ammunition for '84."
         Christian Science Monitor 17 November 1983: 3.

11-43.   "House Fails to Approve ERA." Washington Post 16 November
         1983: A1.

11-44.   "House Panel Approves ERA Without Working Revisions."
         Washington Post November 1983: A4.

11-45.   "House Rejects ERA Measure in 278-147 Vote." Wall Street
         Journal 16 November 1983: 2.

11-46.   "House Swiftly Kills Bid to Revive ERA." Los Angeles Times 16
         November 1983: I, 1.

11-47.   Jones, A. "Politics for the Post-ERA Era." Progressive
         October 1982: 15-16.

11-48.   "Killing ERA Didn't Cure the Patient."   Christianity Today 17
         September 1982: 14.

11-49.   Kulp, D. E.   "ERA Not Dead Yet."   Off Our Backs January
         1984: 8.

11-50.   "Let Them Eat Quiche; Pro-ERA Senators Get a Taste of the
         Stuff."   Washington Post 26 January 1983: B1.

11-51.   Lloyd, K. et al.   "Looking Ahead: Nine Top Women Eye the
         Future."   Working Woman December 1982: 116-120.

11-52.   McClory, R. J.   "ERA Advocates 'Angry, Dejected.'"   National
         Catholic Reporter 2 July 1982: 2.

11-53.   Morganthau, T.   "Politics in a Post-ERA Era."   Newsweek 12
         July 1982: 33.

11-54.   "A New Era for ERA."   Fortune 27 June 1983: 55-57.

11-55.   "The New Right and Women."   Christian Century 28 April 1982:
         499-500.

11-56.   "NOW to Meet in Florida, Ending 6-Year Boycott."   New York
         Times 11 May 1983: 8.

11-57.   Oesch, M.   "ERA's Reintroduced."   Off Our Backs March 1983:
         3.

11-58.   O'Hara, J.   "The Fire in ERA's Ashes."   Macleans 12 July 1982:
         30.

11-59.   "Politics in a Post-ERA era."   Newsweek 12 July 1982: 33.

11-60.   "Praise the ERA and Pass the Buck."   Washington Post 2 June
         1983: A21.

11-61.   "Ratification Defeat Leaves Rights Law on Uneven Path."   New
         York Times 27 June 1982: E5.

11-62.   Rawalt, M.   "ERA Shall Rise Again."   Women's Law Journal 68
         (1982): 125-129.

11-63.   "Requiem for the ERA."   Progressive May 1982: 9-11.

11-64.   Reese, T. J.   "Post-Mortem on the ERA."   America 24 July
         1982: 45.

11-65.   "Reviving the Equal Rights Amendment." (Editorial) America 3
         December 1983: 342-344.

11-66.   "Richmond Vigil Reminds Legislators of Defeated ERA."
         Washington Post 16 February 1984: C1.

11-67. "Rules of the Road for a Bumpy ERA Rerun." Los Angeles Times 12 June 1983: IV, 5.

11-68. Schroeder, P. "The Strategic Revival of the ERA in Congress." Ms. February 1984: 104.

11-69. "Schlafly Soldiers on Against the Feminists." Newsweek 28 February 1983: 10-12.

11-70. "Second Round for the ERA." (Editorial) Los Angeles Times 14 November 1983: II, 4.

11-71. Seligman, D. "A New Era for ERA." Fortune 27 June 1983.

11-72. Shalala, D. E. "Why Settle for #2?" Vogue March 1984: 146.

11-73. "Smokescreen Over the House," (Editorial) Los Angeles Times 18 November 1983, sec. II: 6.

11-74. Spring, B. "What Would the ERA Mean for the Nation's Churches and Seminaries?" Christianity Today October 1983: 32-34.

11-75. Strassler, S. and G. Borger. "The Do-Little Congress." Newsweek 28 November 1983: 46.

11-76. "The Time is NOW: Celebrating ERA's Comeback." Washington Post 16 February 1983: B1.

11-77. Toufexis, A. "What Killed Equal Rights?" Time 12 July 1982: 32-34.

11-78. "Trying Again on ERA." (Editorial) Christian Science Monitor 5 January 1983: 24.

11-79. "2 Senators Engage in Hot Discussion on Equal Rights Amendment." (Hatch and Tsongas) New York Times 27 May 1983: A11.

11-80. "Undaunted by Loss on Equal Rights, Women Look to Courts to Curb Bias." New York Times 29 June 1982: 11.

11-81. "U.S. Amendment on Equal Rights Beaten in House." New York Times 16 November 1983: 1.

11-82. U.S. Senate. Impact of the Equal Rights Amendment. (Parts 1 and 2, 1983, S. Hrg. 98-1259). Washington: GPO, 1984.

11-83. "U.S. Women Gaining in Political Clout." Christian Science Monitor 20 July 1982: 1.

11-84. Van Gelder, L. "Electoral Politics or Civil Disobedience?" Ms. January 1983: 38-40.

11-85. Wall, J. M. "The Real Issue for Women is Power (editorial)." Christian Century 27 October 1982: 1067-1068.

11-86. "Was This ERA Defeat Necessary?" (Editorial) New York Times 17 November 1983: 2.

11-87. "Washington: Another Defeat for ERA." Working Women March 1984: 58-62.

11-88. "Weep Not, Dear Ladies." Wall Street Journal 23 June 1982: 26.

11-89. "With ERA Dying, What's Ahead for Women's Groups?" US News and World Report 28 June 1982: 55.

11-90. "With ERA Dead, Even Eleanor Smeal Asks, What NOW?" Wall Street Journal 25 June 1982: 1+.

11-91. "Women Turn View to Public Office." New York Times 28 June 1982: 1.

Appendix: Organizational Resources

The Miller and Greenberg bibliographic study, The Equal Rights Amendment, (Greenwood, 1975), has an extensive organizational list. In 1984, these organizations were asked to supply publications on the Equal Rights Amendment. Below is a list of organizations which responded with relevant information.

American Association of University Women
2201 Virginia Avenue, N.W.
Washington, DC   20037

American Civil Liberties Union
Literature Department
132 West 43 Street
New York, New York   10036

Business and Professional Women's Foundation
2012 Massachusetts Avenue N.W.
Washington, D.C 20036

California Commission on the Status of Women
926 J Street   Suite 1014
Sacramento, Calilfornia   95814

Coalition of Labor Union Women
Center for Education and Research
2000 P Street N.W.   Suite 615
Washington, DC   20036

Eagle Forum
316 Pennsylvania Avenue S.E.   Suite 203
Washington DC   20003

ERAmerica
1525 M Street N.W.
Washington, DC   20005

Ford Foundation
320 East 43 Street
New York, New York   10017

KNOW, Inc.
P.O. Box 86031
Pittsburg, Pennsylvania   15221

League of Women Voters in the United States
1730 M Street, N.W.
Washington, DC   20036

National Organization for Women
425 13 Street, N.W.
Washington, DC   20004

New York Civil Liberties Union
84 Fifth Avenue
New York, New York 10011

Project on the Status and Education of Women
Association of American Colleges
1818 R. Street N.W.
Washington, DC   20009

Religious Network for Equality for Women
National Office
475 Riverside Drive   Suite 830-A
New York, New York   10019

The Woman Activist, Inc.
2310 Barbour Road
Falls Church, Virginia   22043

"Women in Libraries"
American Libraries Association
SRRT Feminist Task Force
50 East Huron Street
Chicago, Illinois   60611

Women's Bureau
United States Department of Labor
Office of the Secretary
Washington, DC   20210

ERAmerica (Washington, DC) lists the following organizations as supporters of the Equal Rights Amendment (1978):

Allied Industrial Workers of America, International Union
Amalgamated Clothing and Textile Workers Union
Amalgamated Meat Cutters and Butcher Workmen of North
          America
American Anthropological Association
American Association for the Advancement of Science
American Association of Law Libraries
American Association of University Professors
American Association of University Women
American Baptist Churches, U.S.A.
American Baptist Women
American Bar Association
American Civil Liberties Union
American College of Nurse/Midwives
American College of Obstetricians and Gynecologists
American Federation of Government Employees
AFL-CIO (American Federation of Labor-Congress of Industrial
          Organization) and affiliated unions
American Federation of Teachers
AFTRA (American Federation of Television and Radio Artists)
AFSCME (American Federation of State County and Municipal
          Employees)
American Home Economics Association
American Jewish Committee
American Library Association
American Medical Women's Association
American Newspaper Women's Club
American Nurses' Association
American Political Science Association
American Psychiatric Association
American Psychological Association
American Public Health Association
American Public Welfare Association
American Society for Cell Biology
American Society for Ethnohistory
American Society for Public Administration
American Society for Women Accountants
American Studies Association
American Theatre Association
American Veterans Committee
American Women in Radio and Television
Americans for Democratic Action
Association for Intercollegiate Athletics for Women
Association for Women in Science
Association for American Women Dentists
Association for Flight Attendants
B'nai B'rith Women
Board of Church and Society of United Methodist Church

Board of Global Ministries of the United Methodist Church
BRAC (Brotherhood of Railway, Airline and Steamship Clerks,
     Freight Handlers, Express and Station Employees)
Catholic Women for the ERA
Center for Social Action, United Church of Christ
Child Welfare League of America
Christian Feminists
Christian Church (Disciples of Christ)
Church of the Brethern
Church Women United, National Executive Committee
Citizens' Advisory Committee on the Status of Women
CLUW (Coalition of Labor Union Women)
Common Cause
CWA (Communication Workers of America)
Conference of College Composition and Communication
Council of Chief State School Officers
Council of Nurse Researchers of the American Nurses'
     Association
Council of Women and the Church, United Presbyterian
     Church
Democratic National Committee
District of Columbia Area Feminist Alliance
Division 29 "Psychotherapy"of the American Psychological
     Association
Economists in Business
Evangelicals foe Social Action
Executive Women in Government
Family Services Association of America
Federally Employed Women
Federation of Organizations for Professional Women
Federation of Shareholders in American Business, Inc.
Friends' Committee on National Legislation
General Assembly of the Unitarian-Universalist Association
General Assembly of the Unitarian-Universalist Women's
     Federation
General Federation of Women's Clubs
Girl Scouts of the U.S.A.
Grey Panthers
Housewives for the ERA
Institute of Women Today
Intercollegiate Association for Women Students
International Association of Human Rights Agencies
International Association of Machinists and Aerospace Workers
International Association of Personnel Women
International Association of Women Ministers
International Ladies' Garment Workers Union
IUE (International Union of Electrical, Radio and Machine
Workers)
Latin American Studies Association
Leadership Conference on Civil Rights
Leadership Conference of Women Religious
League of American Working Women
League of Women Voters of the United States
Los Angeles Democratic Central Committee

Lutheran Church in America
Men for ERA
Movement for Economic Justice
National Assembly of Women Religious
NAACP (National Association for the Advancement of Colored
    People)
National Association for Women Deans, Administrators and
    Counselors
National Association of Bank Women
National Association of Colored Women's Clubs, Inc.
National Association of Commissions for Women
National Association of Counties
National Association of Social Workers
National Association of Temple Educators
National Association of Women Business Owners
National Association of Women Lawyers
National Black Feminist Organization
National Catholic Coalition for the ERA
National Center for Voluntary Action
National Coalition of American Nuns
National Commission on the Observance of International
    Women's Year
National Consumers League
National Council for the Social Studies
National Council of the Churches of Christ
National Council of Jewish Women
National Council of Negro Women
National Council of Senior Citizens
National Council of Women of the U.S.
National Council on Alcoholism Association for Women in
    Psychology
National Education Association
National Federation of Business and Professional Women's
    Clubs
National Federation of Press Women
National Federation of Temple Sisterhoods
National Governors' Conference
National Ladies Auxiliary/Jewish War Veterans of the U.S.A.,
    Inc.
National Lawyers Guild
National Organization for Non-Parents
National Organization for Women
National Republican Congressional Committee
National Secretaries Association
National Student Nurses' Association
National Welfare Rights Organization
National Women's Party
N-CAP of the American Nurses' Association
National Women's Political Caucus
Network
Newspaper Guild
The Oil, Chemical and Atomic Workers International Union,
    AFL-CIO
Organization of American Historians

Planned Parenthood Federation of American, Inc.
Popular Cultural Association
Priests for Equality
Republican National Committee
Retail Clerks International Association
Sociologists for Women in Society
Soroptimists International of the Americas, Inc.
Southern Christian Leadership Conference
Speech Communication Association
St. Joan's International Alliance
TWU (Transport Workers Union of America)
Union of American Hebrew Congregations
UAW (United Automobile, Aerospace and Agricultural Workers
    of America)
United Church of Christ, 10th and 11th General Synod
United Indian Planners Association
United Methodist Church
United Presbyterian CHurch, U.S.A.
United States Conference of Mayors
United Steelworkers of America
Western Psychological Association
Women in Communications
Women's American ORT
Women's Bureau, Department of Labor
Women's Campaign Fund
Women's Caucus of the National Aid and Defender Association
Women's Division of the United Methodist Church
Women's Equity Action League
Women's International League for Peace and Freedom
Women's National Democratic Club
Women's Ordination Conference (Catholic)
Young Women's Christian Association
Zero Population Growth, Inc.
Zonta International

Janet Boles in The Politics of the Equal Rights Amendment
(Longman, 1979) provides the following list of national and state
organizations opposed to the Equal Rights Amendment:

American Conservative Union
American Independent Party
American Legion (MN)
American Party
American Women Against Ratification on ERA
American Women Already Richly Endowed
Arkansas Women Against the ERA
Christian Crusade

Citizens Against ERA (OH)
Citizens Against the Draft (FL)
Citizens Organized for the Protection in Education of Children
    (OH)
Committee for Retention and Protection of Women's Rights (MS)
Committee to Expose the Equal Rights Amendment (IN)
Committee to Preserve Women's Rights (TX)
Committee to Repeal the ERA (TX)
Communist Party, U.S.A.
Concerned Parents Committee (WS)
Congress of Freedom
Daughters of the American Revolution
Daughters of the Colonial Wars (VA)
Equal Rights Amendment Steering Endeavor (IN)
Farm Bureau (VA)
Federation of Republican Women's Clubs (AL, CT, FL)
Females Opposed to Equality
Feminine Anti-Feminists (OH)
General Federation of Women's Clubs (VA, IL)
Gi Gi Gals Galore Against the ERA (FL)
Grandmothers United Against the ERA (OH)
Happiness of Motherhood Eternal
Happiness of Womenhood
Home Administrators, Inc.
Homemakers' United Efforts (AZ)
Housewives and Motherhood Anti-Lib Movement (OH)
Humanitarians Opposed to Degrading Our Girls (UT)
International Anti-Women's Liberation League
Iowa Women Against the ERA
John Birch Society
Ku Klux Klan
Leadership Foundation
League for the Protection of Women and Children (MO)
League of Housewives
League of Large Families
Liberty Lobby
Minnesota T (Taxpayer) Party
Minnesotans Against the ERA
Montana Citizens to Rescind the ERA
National Coalition for Accountability
National Committee of Endorsers Against ERA
National Council of Catholic Laity
National Council of Catholic Women
National States Rights Party
Parents of New York United
People Leadership (FL)
Pro America
Protect Our Women (WI)
Rabbinical Alliance of America
Rabbinical Society of America
Repeal ERA (NE)
Restore Our American Republic (OH)
Revolutionary Union (WI)
Right to Life (MN, KN)

Right to Be a Women (IL)
Scratch Women's Lib (CT, IN)
Society for the Christian Commonwealth
Stop ERA
Union Women's Alliance to Gain Equality (CA)
United Conservatives of Indiana
Viva La Difference Committee
We the People
Winsome Wives and Homemakers (WI)
Wisconsin Legislative and Research Committee, Inc.
Women Against the Draft (FL)
Women for Constitutional Government
Women for Maintaining the Differences Between the Sexes and
Against the ERA (WY)
Women for Responsible Legislation
Women of Industry
Women Opposed to ERA (KN)
Women United to Defend Existing Rights (NY)
Women Who Want to Be Women
Women's Committee to Rescind the ERA (KY)
Women's Freedom Fund (NY)
Wyoming Women for Privacy and Against the ERA
Young Americans for Freedom

Author Index

Subject Index

About the Compiler

RENEE FEINBERG, Associate Professor of Library Science at Brooklyn College, City University of New York, compiled *Women, Education, and Employment*. She has contributed articles to *The ALA Yearbook*, *Library Journal*, and the *Journal of Research and Development in Education*.